Light From the Other Side

Light from the Other Side

*The Paranormal as Friend and Familiar
(Real Life Experiences of a Spiritual Pilgrim)*

J. Harold Ellens

RESOURCE *Publications* · Eugene, Oregon

LIGHT FROM THE OTHER SIDE
The Paranormal as Friend and Familiar (Real Life Experiences of a Spiritual Pilgrim)

Copyright © 2011 J. Harold Ellens. All rights reserved. Except for brief quotations in critical publications or reviews, no part of this book may be reproduced in any manner without prior written permission from the publisher. Write: Permissions, Wipf and Stock Publishers, 199 W. 8th Ave., Suite 3, Eugene, OR 97401.

Resource Publications
An Imprint of Wipf and Stock Publishers
199 W. 8th Ave., Suite 3
Eugene, OR 97401
www.wipfandstock.com

ISBN 13: 978-1-60899-962-0

Manufactured in the U.S.A.

All scripture quotations, unless otherwise indicated, are taken from the Holy Bible, New International Version®, NIV®. Copyright ©1973, 1978, 1984 by Biblica, Inc.™ Used by permission of Zondervan. All rights reserved worldwide.

*To Mary Jo for compelling me by her persistent example
to open my mind to a wide world of alternative spirituality*

*To Deborah Lynn for probing the far reaches of that world
of alternate spirituality and describing articulately
its vital contours*

*To Jacqueline for living out an honest and inquiring alternative
spirituality without shutting her eyes to her family
traditions or any others*

*To Rebecca for turning her pursuit of alternative spiritualities
into an applied mode of creative life, and teaching it
all over the world*

*To Brenda for not losing her grip on her pursuit of meaningful
spirituality and hope, despite her life being wracked
with unacceptable suffering;
and, nonetheless, bringing the blessings of her spirit to the world
of God's beautiful animal creatures, where divine
spirit is evident everywhere.*

Contents

Foreword by F. Morgan Roberts ix
Preface: Spiritual Autobiography xiii
Acknowledgments xix

1 Introduction: Trauma and Illumination 1
2 How Abnormal is the Paranormal 10
3 The Permeable Screen 25
4 A View from the Bridge 39
5 Sailing Close to the Wind 47
6 Appointments with God 65
7 A Voice in the Night, Truth Quests and Consolations 76
8 The Presence 93
9 Corollary Bible Stories 104
10 Mystical Spirituality 118
11 The Mystics and the Epitome of Mysticism 139
12 The Wisdom Book 144
13 Conclusion 153

Bibliography 157
Subject/Name Index 161

Foreword

If you know that you're human and yearn to enjoy all the possibilities of what it means to be even more fully human, this book is for you. It's not trying to sell you anything; it's about a spiritual inheritance that is already yours to enjoy. It is not the typical book about paranormal experiences. Instead, it's about a larger world of the spirit that already surrounds your life and about all the ways in which that other world has been touching and seeking to infuse your life with deeper meaning. If you're open to a journey that will be constructively life-changing, this book can be your guide upon such a pilgrimage.

To make such claims for any book may seem somewhat remarkable; however, this book is notable in several ways. One of its unusual features is the author himself. Having read rather extensively in the general fields of spirituality and the paranormal, I can say that J. Harold Ellens is not the kind of author that one ordinarily comes upon in such literature. His life experience is importantly diverse; he has lived several lives.

You can address Harold Ellens in a variety of ways. You can call him Professor because he is a university professor, classical and biblical scholar, author, co-author, or editor of 180 books and 168 professional journal articles. Or you can call him Dr. Ellens because he is a practicing psychotherapist. Still yet, you can call him Pastor because he has served 15 congregations. Others have addressed him as Chaplain when he was Colonel Ellens, U.S. Army. Most important of all is that, throughout his varied career, he has enjoyed a rich experience of the divine spirit in his daily life—and in this book he wants you to enjoy that same life-enhancing experience.

You don't have to be religious to find nourishment in this book. For that matter, this is not a religious book in the usual, institutional sense; it does not espouse the doctrines and tenets of a particular religious tradition. So don't stop reading if you're not a traditionally religious person. However, if you are Christian, Jewish, Muslim, Buddhist, or of some other faith tradition, that's O.K. too because this book will enrich your life within your own tradition. This author is not trying to fix or change your mind about religion. Instead, there's something deeper awaiting you in these pages; this book just might baptize your imagination. So this is a book about your life, anyone's life, and how the universal divine spirit is already touching your life in ways you haven't realized, but can learn to recognize and appreciate even more.

As you move through the pages of this book, you will suddenly realize that some of the experiences described by the author are surprisingly similar to things that have happened to you. But you never told anyone about these experiences; you thought that your friends wouldn't understand, or that they might write you off as one of those somewhat strange spiritual seekers who are a bit "loosely wrapped." You yourself may have suspected the sanity of your own interpretations of these events, and so you filed them away in a secret drawer of your mind labeled "happenstance" or "awaiting further light." Even now, as I remind you of these events, you are remembering that, even if they seemed pure coincidence, one such event produced a major turning point in your personal life or career. You just "happened" to be at a certain place at a certain time, and if you hadn't been there just then, your life wouldn't be what it is today.

Even if you called it nothing more than good luck, just remembering it as you read these words reminds you of what an extraordinary "accident" it was. For that matter, it may even have seemed at the time to be very bad luck; however, you know now that it was the best piece of bad luck that could ever have befallen you, because it saved you from taking the wrong road, delaying you just long enough so that you were, later on, at the right place at the right time for something wonderful—so wonderful that you could never even have planned it by yourself. Could it be that these accidents were moments of truly amazing grace, sent into your life from a wholly other, higher world of the divine spirit?

Others reading these words have had still another kind of experience. It often happens in moments of danger, darkness, or distress when they have given up hope. They have sensed a friendly Presence that has come to them, uninvited not sought, accepting them without judgment, invisible yet more visible than what can be seen, a voice unheard but crystal clear, assuring them that all shall be well. Millions of other people have experienced this Presence; their stories need to be heard and pondered. Harold Ellens has sensed that same Presence since his childhood;

and his story in this book will help you to think more deeply about that grace-filled Presence that came to you in your moment of profound need.

Still others have had moments of the Spirit on perfectly good days when everything was going well in their life. They weren't even looking or hoping for anything more in life, but suddenly it was there. Their experience was like that of C. S. Lewis who, awaiting a train late on a glorious October afternoon when "the hills beyond the Dorking Valley were of a blue so intense as to be nearly violet and the sky was green with frost," picked up by chance a book to read for the weekend and, several hours later, knew that he had crossed a great frontier into another world of the spirit. People with everything in their lives proceeding perfectly have been surprisingly refreshed by a gentle breeze that seems to come from another world, whispering words of a deeper, stronger, quieter life into their inner being. Those who have sensed this holy wind that blows into our lives at unsought moments seem to experience something that "church religion" could never have produced—something like a new birth. We seldom share our stories of such moments, but ordinary people of all faiths (or no faith at all) have experienced these winds of the divine spirit. Here is a book in which we can begin to learn to set our sails close to the wind and let the little ship of our lives be carried homeward to our full selfhood by that unseen current of the spirit.

No book can manipulate the winds of the spirit. "The wind blows where it chooses, and you hear the sound of it, but you do not know where it comes from or where it goes." However, you can walk those shores or climb those high hills where it gusts with greater frequency. Here is a book that can take you to those places of likely encounter with that other world that has always surrounded your life, seeking to lead you into the richness, wonder, and variety of all that your life is meant to be.

F. Morgan Roberts,
Palmetto, Florida
June 10, 2010

Preface

Spiritual Autobiography

FIVE YEARS AGO A friend of mine, Dean Streck, ask me to write what he called, "Your Wisdom Book." He explained that he wished me to write a book describing what I had learned in my nearly eighty years of life, learning, and scholarly reflections. He said that he wanted to know what things a man ended up knowing or being certain of, after giving his life for so many years to Christian ministry, and biblical and psychological scholarship. I spent my adult life in full time university work and full time ministry, in congregations and in my psychotherapy clinic - all at the same time. Dean wanted to know what I had figured out.

I thought his request was a good idea, but I did not write the book because I did not then feel quite ready to write such a book. The idea needed to cook for a while in my psyche, and I had to get some other things done first. However, my friend's urgings hung heavily in my heart and head, and persisted as an urgent mandate I would need to attend to eventually. While we do not see each other regularly, our friendship is warm and has survived for two decades.

Recently he sent me an email about new developments in his life, and my sense of his presence and his long standing request put the matter back into center focus. The moment was precisely opportune. His email caught me in the middle of reflection on the truth perceptions and spiritual insights I had gained over the years. I have recently been very interested in, and published a set of three volumes on, matters related to paranormal ways of knowing. That was always of great interest to Dean and to me because I have experienced dramatic, life-changing, paranormal experiences throughout my life.

Dean's urging prompted me to proceed immediately to write the book on the paranormal experiences of my life. I recognize that this is my Wisdom Book for now, prepared in a new and fresher form than would have been possible for me five years ago. This present work is the fulfillment of Dean's request. I wish in this volume to distill, as well as I can, the facts and meanings of the paranormal or parapsychological experiences that have definitively shaped my life from its early moments. At the same time I hope to set down some of the important truth of which I am convinced after a life time of intense study, hard intellectual and spiritual work, and careful analytical attention to the critical experiences that have arisen in this process.

To write such a book as this requires the willingness to unveil the intimacies of an authentic spiritual autobiography. The idea of my writing an autobiography was first broached to me by Henry J. Stob, my mentor and beloved professor during my time at Calvin College and Theological Seminary. He was well acquainted with the fact that my life's pilgrimage had begun in a rural Dutch ghetto in the woods of northern Michigan, had taken me through years as an army chaplain, and had landed me in my vocation as a pastor, therapist, and university professor. He had also read my books and I had edited two of his, as well as his unpublished volume of personal aphorisms. In his dying year he insisted that it was necessary for the community that I write my autobiography.

I was less convinced than he. It was difficult for me to believe anyone would really care to read my life story. Moreover, I could not imagine how it should be crafted. I thought I might write it as a simple annotated catalogue of major events and turning points in my development, but that seemed superficial and boring. I reflected on writing it as Gore Vidal wrote his two volumes, or as Dominick Dunne had written all his life stories. Both had chosen a quasi-novel form of narrative, Gore in the first person and Dunne as a fictional narrator reporting on Dunne's life experience, cast in terms of real life characters, but with fictional names.

Then again, I thought that perhaps an historical novel might be the form to give a properly entertaining autobiography. When all these ideas seemed inadequate I resorted to the idea of just providing a narrative description of my life, as I remembered it, elaborated with the meaning I understood it to have acquired along the way. I sensed that such a presentation could simply follow an approximately chronological pattern. That should be relatively uncomplicated, straight-forward, and honest. That brought me back to the conviction that no one would really care enough about me to read such a story; particularly because it did not seem to me that anything about me was important or useful enough to prompt a self-respecting reader to spend any significant time or thought reading it; to say nothing about actually going out to Borders' Book Store or clicking up Amazon to buy the damn thing. Moreover, I was sure such a book would seem to be too filled with the first personal pronoun all over the place: nothing but I, I, I and me, me, me. That did not sound appealing to me. In fact, it gave me a distinct abdominal sensation that reminded me of my nasty childhood experiences of vomiting all over myself.

So I never got going on an autobiography. Then Dean came along and once again I was being probed and pushed to tell my story. This time, however, it seemed to have a better reason to it. Perhaps it would be of some use for me to tell the story of the way in which my personal spiritual journey unfolded over the years, particularly as shaped by uninvited paranormal experiences that changed my life radically; and that could be accounted for only as breakthrough events of divine illumination: intimations of the Holy Spirit. It would be one facet of the story of what life has come to mean to me over the decades; and why and how it acquired the meanings that it has for me today.

So here it is, for better or worse. I hope, of course, it will be enjoyable and profitable to anyone who picks it up. To make a spiritual autobiography enjoyable and profitable, it seems to me, requires telling the story simply and authentically, as well as starkly and colorfully. That is a challenge I welcome. Those of you who have read my published works know that is my style. For your sake let us hope it comes across that way in this work. Writing autobiographically is always an intimate unveiling of one's self, and a spiritual autobiography requires great sensitivity on the part of the writer and the reader, since it gets "very close to the bone," so to speak.

When we are 13 or 14 year old youths we are quite anxious about two things, mainly, sex and spirituality. If you shout the work "sex" or the word "god" at a 14 year old boy his reaction is approximately the same level of anxiety in both cases. At 14 we are anxious about both because we are equally mystified by both, and both are equally unknown and inaccessible to us. Hence both are to some extent a threat in the sense that the unknown is usually anxiety inducing; and both are inescapable. We must think of both, deal with both, come to terms with both, though we are thoroughly unequipped to deal with either. Sexuality and spirituality are complicated worlds and exploring those unknown worlds so as to understand them, learn to negotiate them well, and come to terms with them, is a tricky business in life.[1]

The reason sexuality and spirituality are both so anxiety inducing in early life lies in the fact that both are so close to the center of who we really are and what we can become, dealing with them makes us feel very vulnerable. In fact, we never completely get over this sense of the intimate sensitivity of our spirituality and sexuality. If a stranger sits next to you on the subway and suddenly begins to tell you her sexual or spiritual life story, you immediately realize her behavior is situation-inappropriate. Her hinges are too loose, psychologically. She seems unaware of the intimate sensitivity such matters deserve.

We are apparently born with the sense that our spirituality and sexuality derive from a force inside us that constitutes our selfhood and defines our natures; it is very close to our center. Therefore, we are by nature very careful about both. We do not easily reveal either. It takes a good deal of work to get to the point that we can truly share our spirituality and sexuality *authentically* with others. Of course, anyone can be pathologically promiscuous, but that requires shearing off our sexual behavior or our spiritual expressions from our authentic emotional selves, our core personhood. The folks these days who seem to be running around with their genitals hanging out, so to speak, grabbing any and every occasion or opportunity to stimulate them, are living empty lives sexually and spirituality because there is no authenticity to their promiscuous behavior; or deep and enduring gratification in their sexual-spiritual experiences.

That reminds me of the Catholic Nun who was lecturing the adolescents in a girls school. She emphasized that they should avoid sexual play and promiscuity at their age, since an hour of fun could leave them with a lifetime of misery. A voluptuous 17 year old raised her hand and said, "Sister, tell us how to make it last an hour." A wham, bam, thank you ma'am experience, does not do much for anyone at the levels of human experience and relationships that mean anything.

Sexuality and spirituality are two expressions of the same life force in us. They are not two different forces, and contrary to much of the

---

1. Cf. J. Harold Ellens, *Sex in the Bible, A New Consideration* (Westport, CT: Greenwood-Praeger, 2006); and J. Harold Ellens, *The Spirituality of Sex* (Westport, CT: Greenwood-Praeger, 2009).

emphases in both secular and religious communities, they do not stand in tension or contrast with each other. They are one and the same aspect of our personalities. When that life force is expressed ethereally through our psyches it reaches out to the transcendent relationship and we call it spirituality. When it expresses itself though our psyches and is channeled through our bodies it reaches out for connected relationship with other humans and we call it sexuality. In both cases it is the expression of a hunger to be genuinely joined with another person, divine or human, at the most intimate level of which we are capable. This requires the revealing of our real inner selves. That is a deeply intimate and profoundly sensitive union.

To write this spiritual autobiography requires of me utter authenticity and involves for me the risk of that kind of deeply intimate and profoundly sensitive union with those of you who will read it. Moreover, one's spiritual story cannot be told completely without one's sexual story, and vice versa. So this book must be deeply personal, and that means that it requires immense vulnerability on my part, but also on your part, in that, if effective, it will call up in you who read this, deeply honest self-awareness and intimate inquiry into your own spiritual journey.

Your journey will have within it, as mine has had, paranormal experiences that you have ignored or suppressed because you did not know what they were, did not know what to call them, did not know anyone to tell about them, and so you did not keep track of them. As you read my story, you will see that some of them were authentic encounters with the divine spirit, and that the screen between the divine world and our daily life is much more permeable than you thought. God is a "friend that sticks closer than a brother."[2]

---

2. Proverbs 18:24.

Acknowledgments

I WISH TO THANK Dean Streck, for motivating me to undertake the project, my longstanding and congenial colleague, F. Morgan Roberts for encouraging me on, guiding me through infelicities and inadequacies in the text, and writing a very kind Foreword to recommend this work. I cannot adequately thank my dear friend of the last couple decades, Beuna Carlson, who keeps telling me what a good book this is and who found all the typos in the text. I thank the ingenious divine spirit for illumining me and seeing me through this work without allowing me to lose the feeling that it is deeply worthwhile.

1

Introduction

Trauma and Illumination

AT TEN O'CLOCK IN the morning of August 3, 1937 I was standing by the well on our small Michigan farm. I remember feeling the intense pleasure of the mid-summer sun and the beauty of our yard and blossoming world. I was five years old. I do not know what I was thinking about, vaguely conscious of my mother's image through the kitchen window; but I remember I was deep in contemplation. I was also longing to run across the country road and up the neighbor's sandy driveway to play with Esther.

She was a blond, blue eyed beauty, also five at the time. We were madly in love. She had been born in April of 1932 and I in July. Neither of us remembered when we started to know each other or when we fell in love. The thought or question simply never came up. I think now that we did not remember any time in life when the other was not there, nor considered that fact to be a thing to think about. We were oblivious of any such idea and sure that we would simply always be there in each other's lives. As in the infinite tranquility of all happy and well cared for children, whose lives are secure, no other possibility ever arose. We were madly in love. We thought it wholly natural. I guess you would say that we simply took it for granted, as confident and trusting children do.

Esther and I spent a lot of time together that summer. We played in the sand and grass on sunny days like this one; or in each other's homes if our mothers forbid us to splash barefoot in the puddles when it rained. We talked all summer about starting school in the fall. School was the East Side Christian School, a mile across the forests and meadows of the farmlands. We assumed we would walk together across our farm, through my grandfather's forest and meadow, and then through the Hendricks' woods and fields to the one-room schoolhouse. Neither of us had visited the school but we knew that all the important people we loved went there and seemed to like it. They were mainly my older brother, and her eight siblings. There was nothing to fear in the forests and meadows and those who had gone before us had trod a clear enough path for at least as far as we had ever explored.

In any case we had every reason to feel completely trusting about our life and its opportunities, and I doubt that either of us had ever really had anything to fear. My mother had been sick quite often during my first five years, so I remember feeling some grief and loss about her absences, but that was largely overlaid with the warm care with which my aunts Sena, Betty, and Gertrude embraced me. They were a constant cherishing presence. When my mother was well she was very warm to me; and my father was consistently, by a wide margin and without any exception, just the very best man I ever came to know. They were both full to overflowing of love and grace.

Esther's home was equally rich emotionally, and exceptionally secure. Except for my older and immediately younger brothers, my siblings had not yet been born. Esther was the last of nine children, a number of them already nearing adulthood. She was part of a tribe of people who loved her and thought she was just the most beautiful jewel ever born. With complete assurance, I thought so too.

Moreover, we trusted God. Both of us were growing up in intensely pious homes in which our fathers' prayers and Bible readings, our mothers singing Psalms and Hymns while they worked, and three deeply meaningful worship services on Sunday, were standard spiritual fare. I am surprised, in retrospect, how much I already got out of the long Sunday sermons every week, two in English and one in Dutch. I think we do children a great disservice today in taking them out of the worship services for Church School just before the preacher starts to preach. We had no Sunday School. Soon after five years of age we started Catechism every Saturday morning, walking the two and a half miles to church for the class. But I am still surprised at the extent to which I, fortunately as it turned out, had grasped the main lines of Christian truth by that fateful day in August of 1937.

I think Esther and I felt much alike on the matter of trusting the love and care of God in our lives. It seemed to simply be the way things were. Nurtured in warm and loving Christian homes, where the sense of the presence of God was immanent in everything, there seemed no other possibilities. God was in his heaven and all was right with the world. That was clear from the way the cattle supplied our milk and meat, the pigs littered and produced food and cash, and the chickens laid lots of eggs. It was the middle of the Great Depression with its largely barter economy, as everyone knows, so we set the five gallon can of cream and the case of eggs at the road side every Friday morning. By noon the grocery man came for them and left three large boxes of food for the week. Things worked like clockwork so far as a five year old could tell. Moreover, the fields flourished. I remembered some years when my father delighted in the fact that we got more potatoes per acre than we used to get; and the meadows and grain fields produced more than enough food for the animals for all winter long.

The Great Depression had some painful aspects to it for our parents, but as five year olds I do not think we were aware of being poor. We did not know that we were deprived because we had no inside plumbing except a water pump, no hot water except what we heated on the kerosene stove, and no wash tubs or bath tubs. Our parents had no luxuries, but we did not know there were such things. Our mothers made our clothes but we thought that was because they loved us and liked to do it. I am sure we got that right. While there was no cash around I doubt that either Esther or I were aware of that. I did not know until years later, for example, that my mother had all those years wished for a wrist watch and some jewelry. I was not aware of the import of my father never having a wedding ring and my mother not getting hers repaired when the opals fell out.

Esther and I were secure, happy, and playfully in love, as children can be in innocent joy.

Whatever it was that I was thinking about that bright summer forenoon by our well, I remember only that it seemed important and interesting at the time. What I do remember was that I was sort of spending time waiting for Esther to appear in the Van Houten yard, so I could run over and play with her. I felt infinitely joyful, delightfully pleased. Surely all was right with God's world in which we were privileged to live.

It was just at that point that I heard the screen door slam on the Van Houten farm house. I remember distinctly how my heart leaped, how I turned with excitement to see that little beauty, Esther. There she stood, at the top of the driveway, looking absolutely terror-stricken, and completely on fire. She burned to death right there before my face. I screamed for my mother, while Esther's frilly summer dress and her beautiful golden hair flamed up into a ball of fire enveloping her. My mother ran to her but there was nothing she could do in those primitive days in that rural Dutch ghetto in the woods of Northern Michigan, such a long way from everything.

Esther died. My life stalled out and ended, there and then. A shroud of palpable darkness descended over me like a heavy black blanket drawn down over my head. It drew down over my eyes, and tangibly descended until it closed in on my whole self, and the lights of my mind and memory went out—completely.

I have no idea now who I was before Esther died; no idea of who I would have been had we gone on growing up in the security of that childhood world and of our mutual affection. I have no clue how it would have been to continue to savor the flavor of our spritely joy and the resilient delights of our fond friendship. It is still too painful to allow myself to deeply contemplate. I try sometimes, but I cannot quite get near it. The dear Esther I knew is gone, and so am I.

I have no memory at all from that day forward for two solid years, except the death of my infant brother in our home a few months later. It strikes me today that he may well have been a casualty of my mother's trauma at the death of Esther. But I do not know because I cannot remember a thing from those two dark years of solid blackness in my mind and soul and world. That was a total and terrible end for Esther and for me. Esther was gone and I was lost in the blackness of some unconscious, unfeeling hell. Perhaps unfeeling is not the right word. My brother says that to his great exasperation, I cried all day every day for the first six weeks of school. Perhaps! I have no memory of any such thing. The person I had known myself to be was not there. I never found him back.

When I came out of that cloud of darkness two years later, it was sudden and dramatic. I had nothing to do with it. It just happened. It was another bright summer day. Out of the dimness of the horse stable I stepped through the barn door into the intense light of the mid-day sunshine and I was immediately embraced and infused with a translucent cocoon of light. It seemed to embrace me, elevate me, and illuminate every corpuscle of my body, mind, and spirit. I felt it throughout my entire self, as though I were caught up in an aura of light, different from and brighter than the summer sunlight all around. It seemed like a thing in itself, shining around me, shining within me, shining through me, an elevating and transcendent illumination. Its meaning was instantaneously completely transparent to me and utterly concrete. I was filled with the most joyful sense that my entire life from that moment on would overflow with the gratifying meaningfulness of caring for all those who seemed to be suffering so abjectly all around me. It was the Great Depression and children were constantly dying in our community.

To spend my life caring for the suffering was not a conclusion to which I came as a result of some revelation or insight that this ecstatic moment conveyed to me. It was not something I did or came to realize under the circumstances. It was a completely new sense of reality with which my whole being was thoroughly infused in that instant of illumination. It was as though an other-worldly light irradiated my whole being, infusing it with an entirely new sense of everything. I do not know how long this sense of being caught up in that elevated state lasted. However, my sense of destiny, realized in that experience, has persisted in a straight line from that moment to this minute. I have never felt inclined to second-guess it. I have pursued it with vigor and clarity. I have sought out the difficult places of human suffering as my place of vocation. I have never considered an alternative.

It is clear to me that my experience of this definitive life-changing event at age seven can not be accounted for in any other way than as a special intervention of God. It was a deliverance from two years of psycho-spiritual imprisonment of my deepest inner self, in such a place of utter hopelessness and helplessness as to have shut down all of my conscious mental and spiritual function. I can only say that during those two years I must have been getting on from one day to the next on automatic pilot. I must have functioned as an automaton.

When the divine spirit, which I now believe is the life-force that pervades every aspect of the universe, intervened to free me, that spirit also in that same moment, instantaneously filled me with a complete, and completely meaningful, clarity about my life's purpose. God set me free and gave me a complete map of my destiny. It was such a comprehensive intimation of my vocation; and such a total illumination of my whole self that it formed me into a completely new person then and there. The entire package was in that moment present inside me. It empowered me as a healthy focused agent with an exceedingly pleasing sense of who I really now am. I also knew immediately that the manner and style in which I would pursue that destiny was as a preacher and pastor in spiritual and social ministry to those who would need me.

I have reflected frequently upon the fact that I knew in that moment that I would study to become a pastor and preacher. The Reverend John L. Shaver was the pastor who had baptized me and continued to serve our congregation until I was twelve. I honored him highly as a really good preacher and as a man of great dignity and presence to the people of our church. He seemed to be the only one in our community in those difficult days of the Great Depression who, in an important way, stood above all the trauma that afflicted all of us and was able to be of some useful help.

He had come from somewhere outside our congregation and community. He brought with him useful abilities uncommon to the rest of us. He was able to intervene for suffering people in ways that seemed to count. It seems to me now that it was a natural sense inside me, that this image of empowerment was the one ideal person of service and ministry in my world, for me to emulate.

As a pastor and psychotherapist, I have since wondered whether that immediate sense of vocation would have taken a different course had there been in our community a really proficient and beloved physician. Would I have perceived that event of illumination, that empowered me with a driving sense of destiny, as automatically taking the form of emulating the physician; serving the suffering in the field of medicine? I do not know the answer to that question. What I knew clearly then was that the path before me was in Christian ministry. I knew that immediately. It completely filled my consciousness. There has never been a moment in my life since then at which there has seemed to me to be an alternate option. Nothing ever entailed the sense of satisfaction and authenticity of purpose I have always felt in ministry, from that moment on.

My course seemed set and I went blithely forward, selecting the turns in the road of education that led to my formal study at Calvin College and Theological Seminary. One of the minor moments of reinforcement in my pursuit of this destiny was in my third year of high school. The Principal of Northern Michigan Christian High School asked me whether I really did intend to go into the ministry. He needed to know because in that case he would need to offer in the high school curriculum the two years of Latin, required for college preparation. I had to confirm on the spot what my intentions were. I told him I intended to become a minister. That was the first time that my sense of calling and intent became a public fact. Declaring myself then and there was the crossing of my Rubicon. The die was cast. That changed nothing inside of me, but it advanced the reshaping of my public world and set me on the academic road to ordination.

I enjoyed college and seminary, though having to work full time to support myself often left me feeling like I was not able to do it with the luxuriant freedom and elaborate achievement that I really desired. From my illumination at age seven onward I remained an unfortunately neurotic kid and an adolescent rather lacking in social confidence. I am sure this can be traced to whatever state I was in for the two years of hell following Esther's death.

It was clear to me from high school on, in any case, that if I were to become a really good preacher and teacher I would need to overcome this serious deficit. By sheer force of will I set myself to take every course in rhetoric and public address offered at college and seminary until I felt like my role in the pulpit was second nature to me. It took a few years in pulpit ministry for me to get to the point at which I felt the appropriate confidence. I was always consoled by Cicero's purported remark that if a person were not extremely anxious before making an important speech, he or she was not taking the situation seriously enough. Cicero often had to cancel speaking engagements because he was so overwhelmingly anxious that he could not deliver the address. He is said to have believed that a good deal of anxiety, however, enhances the urgency of ones delivery.

I finished seminary in due season, was ordained to the Christian ministry, and went immediately into the US Army Chaplaincy. My oldest brother had served in WWII and my second brother during the Korean War. I had the sense that the real point of human need at that moment was the young men down on the ground in the mud and blood of war. Moreover, I had a strong sense that if I were to be any good in civilian congregations later, I would need to have a good deal of military experience under my belt, since a majority of the men under my ministry would always be veterans. It was the wise leading of the Lord that teased me down that path. In the direction of that kind of providence, my life in ministry unfolded. I remained on active military duty for nearly ten years and continued very actively involved in the army reserve forces thereafter, completing 37 years of service and retiring as a Colonel in 1992. That experience was one of the most gratifying aspects of my life and of the life of my family.

While serving troops in infantry divisions it became clear to me that the most important facet of my work as a military preacher and pastor was pastoral counseling. That led me to the determination that I needed more training in counseling and in sophisticated biblical studies to increase my usefulness to my people. Calvin Seminary had been extremely deficient in both biblical studies and pastoral counseling in my years of study there. I left the active military service to continue my biblical studies at Princeton Theological Seminary and then to do a PhD in the Psychology of Human Communication at Wayne State University. While pursuing those advanced studies I pastored congregations to support my family. Eventually I finished a PhD in biblical studies at the University of Michigan, as well.

All of this has seemed to me to have developed along a straight line trajectory from God's intervention in my life at age seven, delivering me from a strange psycho-spiritual bondage and empowering me for purpose-driven life. It is one straight line from that moment to this one, in which I am telling you this story of vocation and work in God's human vineyard. People often ask me how I can have done so many different things in life. I have not. I have done only this one thing: I have followed the leading of the divine spirit through a rich and comprehensive ministry to human need in this complex world of human travail. "Life is a tragic adventure," said John F. Kennedy. I know that from the inside, and I have stayed inside that tragic adventure where the real human suffering is and has always been. I believe I have done some definitive good there, as God definitively did good for me on that bright summer morning in 1939.

The import of that great renovation of my life at age seven, as I stepped out through the stable door into the brilliant morning sun, is that it grounded the nature of my person and the trajectory of my vocation in a life-changing paranormal event. It marked out in my life a profound and inerasable awareness that the divine spirit, that is pervasive in the whole world, manifests itself to us naturally in paranormal events that change life. I have never been able to escape that awareness and that certitude. Subsequently my life has been regularly marked by such parapsychological events, equally dramatic, equally illumining, and equally redemptive for me.

Such constructive paranormal experiences are from the divine spirit and the intimations and illuminations of that divine presence are more prevalent than most people are aware. The remarkable uniqueness of such events and the constructive renovation they bring to human lives certifies that they cannot be accounted for in any other way than as the direct interventions of the Holy Spirit of God.

2

How Abnormal is the Paranormal?

CULTIVATING A CULTURE OF THE DIVINE SPIRIT

ONE OF THE THINGS I have most enjoyed doing in my life is teaching university courses in ancient Greek and Roman studies. I teach a course every semester in Greek and Roman Civilization and a course in Greco-Roman Mythology. I always start out each course with an introductory lecture in which I try to define what the Greeks were up to, on which the Romans followed. I argue that from the dawn of their history the Greeks were on a scientific quest to carefully cultivate a civilized culture. Apparently they were already busy with that in their pre-history, for when they appear upon the scene of recorded time, they already had developed a very elaborate mythology. In it they tried to account for the nature and behavior of gods and humans. That was a scientific enterprise in that it was their attempt to create a unified theory of everything, a comprehensive worldview that made their quest for meaning as rational as they could manage at that time.

They called their quest, *Paideia*. The word meant something like the careful quest, through education and rational management of life, to create a civilized culture. It was a surprisingly sophisticated idea for the seventh or eighth century before the time of Julius Caesar, Philo Judaeus, Augustus Caesar, Jesus Christ, and Flavius Josephus. Those ancient folk employed that increasingly rationalizing quest for truth and God from animism to polytheism; and from there to monotheism, landing finally in the time of Socrates, Plato, and Aristotle in what we now call fifth century (BCE) humanism. It was a grand achievement.

However, what I wish to emphasis here is that the Greeks, and the Romans after them, consciously undertook to create a mature, idealized culture of the mind, body, and spirit or psyche. They raised the bar very high for the human quest for beauty, rationality, political order, societal stability, religious wisdom, material wellbeing, and psycho-social comfort. That idea of intentionally creating a culture of high quality for persons and for a society, is an extraordinary notion. To carry it out as well as they did way back then, was quite an amazing achievement. Societies or communities can choose to have an ideal culture that lifts the human spirit toward truth and idealism; or a community can slobber along in a degraded culture that has no idealism and erodes the human spirit.

During most of my life in ministry I have conducted an intentional and concerted work with prisoners. I am well acquainted with what a unique experience prison life is. I have a son-in-law who is an officer at Jackson State Prison. Whenever we discuss his work I become aware again of the fact that the experience of being in prison, for the guards and the prisoners alike, is a special way of life. That is, it takes on the shape of a prison culture. It is a very different, unconventional mode of existence, but it runs as a community system because the conditions are clear to everyone, the expectations are understood by everyone, and that culture has a language peculiar to its community. In a constructive way, the same was true for me for the 37 years I served as an army officer. The military culture in itself was as pleasing for me as the prison culture is horrid for its inhabitants.

Comparably, since the 1970s we have heard a lot of talk about the distinctive kinds of communities in which we live in America. People speak positively or pejoratively about being part of an urban culture or of a suburban culture, of an American culture or of an ethnic culture. Depending upon your value system, you may be pleased or pained by any or all of this. We hear of people bemoaning the loss of America's rural culture or the culture of the family farm. Most people who grew up in rural cultures do not bemoan its disappearance.

I once lived briefly, as a soldier, in Tuckahoe, New York near the Bronx. There I discovered that people in those New York villages of the 1950s each had a distinctive way of life, a culture quite different from what I had experienced elsewhere. One of the striking things about it was that our neighbor and friend from the Bronx was scared to cross the Hudson River into what she considered the Western Wilderness. She was sure that if you crossed the Appalachian Mountains you would find wild Indians riding broncos with feathers stuck in their hair.

During the 1960s, 1970s, and 1980s we heard much about hippie types going back to nature—a naturalist culture. We do not hear of that anymore because most of those experiments failed when those folks, ignorant of what nature was really like, discovered to their dismay that the first chance it gets nature will bite you in the very most sensitive places you have, and will discourage and defeat you in your naive return to primitivity.

I am interested in emphasizing here what it means to create a distinctive way of life or a distinctive kind of culture, in the sense I have just suggested. For 20 centuries Christian churches have been busy cultivating a Jesus culture; and talked all the time about following Jesus, loving Jesus, living Jesus' example, being Jesus' disciples, and working for Jesus. There was a certain remote truth to that, but it is not exactly in line with Jesus' instructions. You will remember from John 14 and 17 that Jesus said, "I am going away. You cannot come now. I will prepare a place for you eternally; but the important thing is that I will send you the Holy Spirit of God who will testify to you regarding what I was up to, and that spirit will lead you into the truth."

The Jesus Culture in the church for 20 centuries turned Jesus into a religious idol and replaced, in our consciousness, both God and God's pervasive divine spirit with an ancient historical Jewish figure, Jesus of Nazareth. Apparently Jesus intended his followers to cultivate a new form of consciousness, namely, a Holy Spirit Culture. By that I mean that everything we think, say, anticipate, hope for, and experience regarding our relationship to God and to the church may be shaped by conscious and intentional awareness of the divine spirit. That means that to be a Christian and to be the church in the world will mean that we expect to experience God present to us in this day and age as spirit. Thus we should always be expecting to experience that presence. Presumably God is always busy trying to relate to us as spirit in our spirits. Apparently we should be far less surprised, than I was, and humans always seem to be, by paranormal events of the intervention of the divine spirit, such as my life-changing epiphany in 1939.

I think that cultivating a culture of consciousness of the divine spirit's pervasive presence in the world and in our personal lives, here and now, means ten things.

> First it means *expecting* to experience the presence of God's spirit in tangible ways regularly.

Second, it means to *hold ourselves consciously open* to the intimations of God's spirit in our daily experiences.

Third, it requires that we *notice* the manifestations of God's spirit in ordinary and extraordinary moments and events.

Fourth, it involves *identifying* those experiences of God's manifestations to us individually and communally as the presence of the divine spirit.

Fifth, it means that we must *name* those moments as "of the spirit."

Sixth, it means that we must *explain* those moments to each other and thus raise the consciousness level of us all regarding the constant ministry of the spirit in our lives.

Seventh, it involves *continually recalling* together that those moments have happened and continue to happen.

Eighth, it means to become a community of believers who are *constantly conscious* that we are experiencing God's spirit all the time.

Ninth, it requires that we *develop an aura* of consciousness of being the people who live in the matrix of the active presence of God's spirit in us and around us.

Tenth, it means coming to *think of ourselves* as the community which is constantly made lively by that spirit of God.

That is what I mean by creating a Holy Spirit Culture, cultivating a consistent consciousness of the presence of divine agency palpably operative in human experience. We do not need to do anything to make it happen except to cultivate a constant consciousness of the experiences of the divine spirit's presence to us. You could say that we live in a matrix of forces that looks natural but is in fact supranatural. God is always working by the spirit, from the eternal world, into this temporal world. The spirit of God is alive here. You all have stories to tell that testify to that.

When we 1) notice those kinds of moments, 2) name them for what they are, and 3) celebrate them together, we become a culture conscious of the spirit. They are not always such dramatic experiences as I experienced in 1939; but they always constructively change one's life. It may be an inadvertent meeting with a stranger in the grocery store line that turns into an illumining moment of sharing important spiritual insight, heartening your life for the rest of the day. Every time, however, whether a great or small event, it is the breaking in of the presence of God's spirit into our spirit's consciousness, to enhance our lives with a light from heaven. We need to remember those moments and make them a part of the growing consciousness of the fact that we live in that kind of supranatural world of the spirit that participates already now in the things eternal.

It is interesting that in present day human culture we do not have a greater awareness than we do of the frequency with which humans experience life-changing paranormal events. There are almost certainly two primary reasons for that. First, within the religious communities of the Western World, namely, Judaism, Christianity, and Islam, the dogmatic and doctrinaire standardization of what should be believed as religious truth and what should be expected as spiritual experience has been largely prescribed. One would think, upon reflection, that religious communities would be particularly interested in the frequency and meaning of paranormal experiences that constructively change people's lives and enhance their understanding of their own spirituality. It is the case, however, that the prescribed nature of most religious life squelches the openness humans have toward the reality and importance of their paranormal experiences.[1]

Second, paranormal experiences are very difficult to describe, define, and fully comprehend. Since they are so mysterious and uniquely personal, we are all quite hesitant to report our "otherworldly" experiences, lest we be considered at least strange and at worst psychopathological. Nonetheless, persons generally have such paranormal experiences which are unlikely to be adequately accounted for, except as personalized moments of spiritual illumination effected by the divine spirit that pervades all facets of our mundane world. As I indicated in the previous chapter, my earliest life changing paranormal experience that I can recall happened when I was seven years of age. I never shared that event with anyone until I was twenty five years old, and then I only told it briefly to a physician. Such definitively shaping experiences continued to happen in my life on a relatively regular basis. However, I never shared those

---

1. Stanislav Grof, Healing Potential of Spiritual Experiences: Observations from Modern Consciousness Research, Vol. 3, *Personal Spirituality*, Ch. 7 in J. Harold Ellens, ed., *The Healing Power of Spirituality, How Faith Helps Humans Thrive*, 3 vols. (Santa Barbara, Denver, and Oxford: ABC-CLIO Praeger, 2010), 131.

with anyone until I began to write about them and mention them in lectures and sermons after my seventieth year.

If you asked me why I began to address this part of my life in my eighth decade of life, I suppose I would say that four things conspired to prompt it. First, I finally had the zeal, time, and energy to try to figure out what was going on in those paranormal experiences and why they were so life-altering in each case. Second, I wanted to know why, in my case, they were always so beneficial in the changes they spontaneously brought about, without my cooperation or agency. They always came to me. I did not seek them. They just happened to me and gave me a different life and personhood, as a result. Third, I find that with age comes a natural desire to put everything about oneself on the top of the table, so to speak—to tell one's full story, since few around one seem to be really catching on to it or care much about it. It seems that especially those one loves the most understand it and search it out the least. Fourth, when I was seventy-one I was finally discovered by significant publishers who were genuinely interested in getting as much of my work as possible and publishing as much about me as they could get. That finally gave me an adequate pulpit or podium from which to tell my story for the benefit of humanity, so to speak.

Not everyone is fortunate enough to be led by such a rich and enriching providence to this kind of opportunity in life. Nonetheless, enriching paranormal experiences are, I believe, happening in everyone's life all the time. However, it takes the eyes to see them, the ears to hear them, and openness of spirit to notice them, so to speak, if one is to recognize them for what they are, take them for real, and celebrate them. Otherwise we tend to dismiss them as weird moments to be quickly repressed and forgotten. I am interested in writing this book for many reasons, but the primary one is to provide the human community a greater sense of freedom and recognition of the reality and importance of our paranormal experiences. This is important to me because I firmly believe that if we keep track of those numinous events, we shall be greatly enriched with a sense of being directly in touch with the divine spirit.

CREATING A SCIENCE OF THE PARANORMAL

Ideas about paranormal human experiences vary as widely as human imagination and popular opinion can stretch. Generally speaking such experiences are viewed with suspicion in our scientific age. That is a very different outlook than one would have found before the Renaissance and Reformation of the sixteenth century. These twin movements led to what we call the Age of Enlightenment, by which we really mean to refer to the scientific revolution, which led in turn to the industrial revolution, the atomic revolution, the technological revolution, and the space age.

However, before these radical sixteenth century changes in western culture, people generally took paranormal experiences seriously and lived largely in terms of them. That is to say, they trusted their intuitions, extrasensory perceptions (ESP), and moments of prescience, when they discerned things that were about to happen and in fact did subsequently take place. They had no reason to question them most of the time. Living by those parapsychological ways of knowing worked for them about as well as living scientifically works for the general human community today. People in those pre-modern times took such experiences for granted, looked for them, longed for them, understood them, knew how to interpret them, kept track of them, and developed a kind of culture in which such experiences were appreciated as leading and shaping their lives—most of the time constructively.

However, the Reformation opened the door of the human mind to the sense that the universe could be understood scientifically, rather than intuitively. That is, it provided the freedom to recognize that the universe operates with consistency and predictability in keeping with specific natural laws. It is tractable, it can be studied profitably by applying the scientific method to all of its aspects. The scientific method had been developed by Aristotle in the 4th century BCE in Greece, but had been largely forgotten in the western world until the Muslim Arabs brought it to our attention again after the age of the crusades. Francis Bacon reformulated it in the mid-fifteenth century CE, for our scientific exploitation.

Most every child in Middle School today knows what the scientific method is. It involves noticing a certain pattern of activity or function in the natural or human world, formulating a hypothesis about what is going on, collecting a lot of data on the issue, and testing the hypothesis against the sample of data. From that one can draw a conclusion that the hypothesis is incorrect and another one needs to be formulated, or that the hypothesis is correct and the data proves that a sound theory can be developed about the phenomenon being studied. Let us say the issue being studied is the question as to whether it is true that water always freezes at 32 degrees and boils at 212 degrees Fahrenheit. Let us say that much data has been collected and we have established that formulating the theory is appropriate.

The scientific method then requires that we test the theory with a data base that is as near to universalizable as possible. If the data again proves that the theory does not always work, it must be discarded or modified. For example, if some of the data is collected at sea level and some at 14,000 feet altitude, that data will demonstrate that the theory holds only at sea level for freezing or boiling water. At 14,000 feet water boils at so low a temperature that you cannot properly boil an egg. Atmospheric pressure is 14.5 pounds per square inch at sea level. The decreased atmospheric pressure at high altitudes allows the water to evaporate or boil at a much lower temperature at those altitudes. So the theory must be modified with the addition of the phrase, "at sea level." Now the theory works accurately. So we apply the theory to general operations and find that it continues to ring true so we declare that it is a law of nature that water always functions in precisely these ways at sea level.

From the 16th century forward this method was applied to every aspect of human experience and produced the series of scientific revolutions named above. Unfortunately, this led the western world to such a preoccupation with the scientific method that we lost our trust in, openness to, and appreciation of those more spiritual or psychic experiences that we now call, consequently, paranormal experiences. We forgot that before the 16th century they were common and were considered normal.

The age of science from the mid-sixteenth to the mid-twentieth century is called the modern era. Fortunately, we now live in an age that is being called the post-modern age. To most people that sounds mysterious and mystifying. However, it may be described rather simply. Postmodern simply means that during the modern era our culture cultivated a devotion to science in a very narrow sense of the word. Science during the modern era meant empirical science, that is, the kind of analysis of things that can be done through the five senses: seeing, touching, smelling, tasting, and hearing. Basically it came down to the study of things that can be measured and weighed or examined in a laboratory. While that empowered science to discover an enormous amount of helpful knowledge about the material world, it limited the scope of science severely. It left out the entire world of the human spirit and of the actions of the divine spirit in history.

Consequently, science of that sort could only study cause and effect issues, but could never approach the analysis of meaning and purpose issues. However, humans have a greater hunger for understanding the meaning and purpose of things than merely the cause and effect of why water boils at 212° Fahrenheit at sea level and only at sea level. That is *nice* to know, but the meaning of life is *necessary* to know to satisfy the irrepressible hunger of the human heart for meaning. That irrepressible hunger is the very definition of spirituality.

Post-modern science is demanding the recognition that the phenomena of human experiences of the psyche, spirit, and transcendent world are also crucial arenas of investigation for better understanding. Moreover, post-modern science wants to find a way to assess the reality, meaning, and value in the fact that such experiences frequently seem very individualized or unique—but nonetheless profoundly real. Post-modernism is asking two questions, among many others. The two that interest me greatly here are "How abnormal is the paranormal?" and "How can we create a science of the paranormal?"

This new type of scientific investigation has been made urgently necessary because of the fact that inadequate cooperation has been achieved, so far, between the contributions that the empirical sciences and the biblical and theological sciences can bring to bear upon the study of paranormal experiences of the ancient world, as well as of our own moment in time. The exact sciences, such as mathematics and chemistry, and the social sciences, such as psychology and economics, have tended to follow a trajectory of investigation in one direction; and the biblical and theological or spiritual sciences have tended along a different track. The former, understandably, follows the avenue of the hermeneutic of suspicion, while the latter, also understandably, follows the avenue of the hermeneutic of analytical but less suspicious and more affirming inquiry.

The virtual absence of pages or sections in professional and scientific journals, even those devoted to religious, spiritual, or theological perspectives, on issues dealing with paranormal human experiences, is most unfortunate. Some attention to these matters is beginning to be afforded by *The Journal for Psychology and Christianity*, *The Journal for*

Psychology and Theology, and the *European Journal of Empirical Theology*, as well as Division 36 of the American Psychological Association.

Of course, the function of peer reviewed journals is to publish replicable research results. However, perhaps a section in each professional journal should be devoted to reporting incidents of the paranormal so that a universe of discourse and a vehicle for discussion could be developed for taking such data into consideration. At present it is not discussed in the scientific realm because no instrument is available for collecting and processing the data. It is important to create a culture of openness to the paranormal experiences humans have, regularly and really, so that the frequency of such events can be understood more clearly, recorded, described, named, categorized, and analyzed.

We may discover, if we create such instruments for raising our consciousness level and increasing our information base, that there are eight things that strike us with surprising urgency. First, we may discover that the incidents of paranormal events are more frequent, should I say more normal, than we think.[2] Second, we may discover that they fit into specific patterns that can be categorized and even analyzed more readily than we have imagined. Third, that may bring to the surface of our thought-processes insights about the nature and sources of paranormal events that are currently ignored because we have not reduced our mystification about them. This may be simply because we have not done the first and second steps above.

Fourth, we may find that the paranormal events are apparently more normal, in terms of the frequency and universality with which humans experience them, than are what we now call normal experiences. Fifth, we may discover that we can establish criteria for sorting out the real from the unreal in what we are now referring to as the mystifying paranormal. Sixth, we may discover that a solicitation of anecdotal reports will produce such a wealth of information as to give rise to an entirely new arena for productive research. If the spirit of God is communicating with our spirits by way of paranormal experiences, presumably it is because God thinks we can hear and interpret the content, making unmystifying sense of it if we study it carefully. This would be a procedure

2. Ralph W. Hood, Jr. and Greg N. Byrom, Mysticism, Madness, and Mental Health, Vol. 3, Ch 9, in J. Harold Ellens, ed., *The Healing Power of Spirituality, How Faith Helps Humans Thrive*, 3 vols. (Santa Barbara, Denver, and Oxford: ABC-CLIO Praeger, 2010), 173.

just like we have used to study the stuff of this world that we have mastered by our empirical science. Seventh, not all truth is empirical data. A great deal of our understanding of the truth about this mundane world we know from phenomenological investigations and heuristic interpretations. These seem to be trustworthy instruments of research that are particularly suited to investigation of the reported experiences humans have of the paranormal. We should be able by means of them to create useful theories, data collection and management systems, hypotheses, and laws regarding the human experiences of the paranormal.

Eighth, if one assumes the existence of God and God's relationship with the material world, immediately a great deal of data is evident within the worldview of that hypothesis, suggesting a good deal of available knowledge about God. Much of this is derived from the nature of the universe itself. Much of the evidence for God's nature and behavior, within that model of investigation, is replicable, predictable, testable, and the like. Why would we not assume the same is true of the world of the paranormal, if we studied it thoroughly and systematically? We call it paranormal only because we have not yet discovered or created a framework of analysis by which its data can be collected and managed.

Some decades ago a great deal was made of chaos theory and entropy in interpreting the unknown aspects of the material world, particularly in the field of astrophysics and cosmology. It turned out that we always think things just beyond our model and grasp or functional paradigm are chaotic. That is only because we do not understand them, not because they are not coherent, lawful, and predictable. We think things just beyond our ken are chaotic because our paradigm is too limited to manage the data out there. Life is always a process of that kind of growth that requires constant expansion of our paradigms.[3] When we cannot expand our paradigm, whether because of our fear or blockheadedness, and so are unable to take in the next larger world of data that we are discovering, we shrink and wither, and our scientific systems go down.

At this very moment we stand upon a threshold demanding an expansion of our scientific paradigm to take in the data of the paranormal in a manner that it can be brought into new, but coherent models of knowledge and understanding. It has been argued that part of the difficulty in studying the spiritual and related paranormal data scientifically lies in the fact that each event is intensely personal and unique. Each

---

3. Robert Fuller, *Religion in the Life Cycle*, (Philadelphia: Fortress, 1988).

scientific exploration of that event must deal with an equation in which n = 1.[4] That makes scientific extrapolations impossible. I suggest, however, that if we undertook the program I propose above, we might well discover that n = much more than 1, and in that case we would be off and running along a trajectory that would teach us how to expand our present limited scientific paradigms to take in the additional real data from the world we now call paranormal merely because we are ignorant of its nature and meaning.Why would we not hypothesize that what is for us the world of the paranormal is really a very normal world of human process about which we may learn a lot more if we look at it more carefully and determine how to assess it systematically. Perhaps we are even warranted in hypothesizing that, from God's perspective, what we call paranormal and, therefore, consider abnormal, is really a normal, functional part of God's world of operations. We may not yet understand that world well; we may be infinitely mystified by it. However, if paranormal events enhance human wellbeing, they are real and of God, since God is God and grace is grace.

The Bible assumes a worldview in which the veil between the mundane and transcendent world is permeable. God seems to move back and forth through that screen rather readily to accomplish specific redemptive actions in this world. We need not adopt that worldview to take seriously the reality of redemptive paranormal human experiences. On the other hand, we should not dispose of that worldview too readily either. Since we do not know a great deal about the transcendent world and the screen that seems to exist between here and there, in all honesty we should keep a mind of open wonder about any and all of the possibilities.

In the September 2007 issue of *Discover, Science, Technology, and the Future*, Jeanne Lenzer published an article entitled Citizen, Heal Thyself.[5] She declares that the sorts of paranormal or miraculous events in the biblical narratives are happening all around us everyday. John Matzke was thirty years old when he was informed that he had terminal melanoma with lung metastasis. The oncologist at the Veterans

---

4. William P. Wilson, How Religious or Spiritual Miracle Events Happen Today, Vol. I, *Religious and Spiritual Events*, Ch 15, in J. Harold Ellens, ed., *Miracles, God, Science, and Psychology in the Paranormal*, (Westport, CT: Praeger, 2008).

5. Jeanne Lenzer, Citizen, Heal Thyself, in *Discover, Science, Technology, and the Future*, September, 2007, 54–59, and 73.

Administration hospital urged immediate surgical treatment, despite the fact that patients with his condition have 50% mortality within two and a half years after surgery. John chose to take thirty days to strengthen his body for the treatment. He spent much time walking in the mountains and forest, meditating, visualizing his healing cells killing the cancerous ones. He concentrated, as well, on eating a healthy diet. When he returned to his physician the doctor expected to see two large lung lesions. Instead the radiographies showed a complete lack of any pathology. The physician said, "When John came back a month later, it was remarkable—the tumor on his chest X-ray was gone. Gone, gone, gone!" He was given eighteen months to live. He lived another eighteen years. Then recurrence of the cancer in his brain killed him.

> Pinning down spontaneous remissions has been a little like chasing rainbows. It's not even possible to say just how frequently such cases occur—estimates generally range from 1 in 60,000 to 1 in 100,000 patients. . . But genuine miracles do exist, and throughout the history of medicine, physicians have recorded cases of spontaneous remission. . . . not just cancer but conditions like aortic aneurysm, . . . Peyronie's disease, a deformity of the penis; and childhood cataracts.[6]

Researchers speculate that Matzke's immune system, reinforced by his change in life style and psychospiritual address to his tumors, produced a healing effect. They noticed that during his month of meditation and healthy living his skin tumors were surrounded by white halo-like rings, indicating that the immune system was attacking the melanocytes, pigmented cells in the skin that give rise to the cancer.[7] Ever since 1700 or so a medical record has been developing indicating that certain serious infections such as erysipelas or those associated with Streptoccoccus, cure cancer by causing tumor regression. It was by following up on these cures which nature spontaneously induces that physicians were able to develop the chemotherapy that is used today. The medical statistics available today indicate that a surprisingly high number of patients are cured or significantly improved in health by both spontaneous remission and by assisting nature through inducing the infectious condition created by chemotherapy.

6. Lenzer, 56.
7. Idem.

Lenzer reports the case of Alice Epstein, a brilliant academic diagnosed with kidney cancer in 1985. A month after the resection of her kidney the cancer showed up in both lungs. Her life estimate at that time was three months.

> Epstein, who says she had a "cancer-prone personality," then turned to psychosynthesis, which she describes as a "combination of psychotherapy and spiritual therapy." It helped her overcome depression, difficulty expressing anger, and suppression of her own needs in order to please others—traits she and some psychologists believe are characteristic of the cancer-prone personality. Although she never received any medical or surgical treatment for the deadly cancer invading her lungs, six weeks after starting psychosynthesis, her tumors began to shrink. Within one year, they had disappeared without a trace. That was 22 years ago.[8]

Today Epstein is alive and well and 80 years of age.

The crucial points at stake here are as follows. First, given the right chance, the irrepressible life force in nature is able to induce spontaneous remission of horrible disorder in the physical organism of human beings. Second, the state of psychospirituality of that person seems to have a great deal to do with the onset of illness and the effecting of cure. Third, a decisive shift in orientation in the psychospiritual world of that person seems to be the trigger that induces radical reorientation of the organic forces at play in the physiological organism, the human body.

Focus upon the permission to be well and not sick, and focus upon the will to get well, is a high priority factor in mobilizing the power of our physiological organism to eliminate the deadly forces that work against the well being of the person. It is clear that this works when the ill person determines to live and be well. One can confidently speculate that a directive to get well, given by an authority whom that sick person respects as a healer, would be enough in some cases to trigger the will to empower the immune system to overcome the pathological and pathogenic condition in his or her body. Why would not the perception and intimation that God intends the patient to be well do the same?

Lenzer concludes almost lyrically. "Although medical advances have dramatically improved outcomes in certain cancers . . . modern medicine has yet to come close to nature's handiwork in inexplicably producing spontaneous remission without apparent side effects for

---

8. Ibid., 58.

people like John Matzke and Alice Epstein, who have experienced the rarest hints of nature's healing mysteries."[9] The interesting question arising in the context of these and modern reports of paranormal events is whether the biblical narratives were attempts to report literal histories of cured persons,[10] or the imagination of the primitive church at work in glorifying their memory of Jesus.[11] Most probably the former!

This question interfaces with our modern perplexity regarding whether the present day life-changing paranormal experiences operate within the same paradigm as those ancient stories or are of a remarkably different order. It is at present too early to tell, but it is surely the scientific imperative for this century to collect the massive data of such human experiences that is apparently available, analyze that data, endeavor to discern patterns and paradigms, and carefully categorize and interpret the meaning of it all. Now it looks like chaos, but we must assume, as in all other scientific breakthroughs in the past, that it is only a chaos in our minds, not in the data; and that if we attend properly to the data, we will see its paradigms and the chaos will turn into scientifically describable order.

There is reason to believe that the paranormal is not really abnormal; while our failure so far to attend to it properly is, indeed, abnormal in this wonderful scientific world.[12]

---

9. Op. Cit., 73

10. Charles Caldwell Ryrie, *The Miracles of Our Lord*, (New York: Nelson, 1984). See also Reginald H. Fuller, *Interpreting the Miracles*, (Philadelphia: Westminster, 1963).

11. Anton Fridrichsen, *The Problem of Miracle in Primitive Christianity*, (Minneapolis: Augsburg, 1972). See also Gerd Theissen, *The Miracle Stories of the Early Christian Tradition*, (Edinburgh: T&T Clark, 1983). Originally published as *Urchristliche Wundergeschichten: Ein Beitrag zur formgeschichtlichen Erforschung der synoptischen Evangelien*, (Gutersloh: Gutersloher Verlaghaus Gerd Mohn, 1974).

12. Parts of the argumentation of this chapter appeared in substantially different form in J. Harold Ellens, *Miracles: God, Science, and Psychology in the Paranormal*, Westport, CT: Praeger, Vol. I, 2008).

3

The Permeable Screen

THE THREE PRIMARY PARAPSYCHOLOGICAL ways of knowing, intuition, ESP, and prescience, are qualities or capacities possessed by all human beings. Some of us have some or all of these ways of knowing to a high degree and some of us to a lower degree. Everyone has had the experience of not having thought of a certain friend for a long time and then out of the blue, so to speak, getting the urge to phone her. Then, just as we are reaching for the telephone to make that call, it rings and it is the person we were intending to ring up. Some would say that is mere coincidence, however, it occurs so often, consistently in the same way, with nearly every person. So it must be acknowledged that this is a universal human capacity to be aware of the thoughts and intentions of another person over a great distance. It is time that we stop merely repressing the awareness of these kinds of experiences of ESP and investigate the nature and function of it and its impact upon our lives.

It is a bit astonishing, is it not, that we would invest rational thought and empirical experience, as ways of knowing, with such absolute veracity as we do; but thoroughly distrust, repress, and devalue these persistent occurrences of remarkably universal paranormal experiences of knowing data that proves to be utterly real and factual. The evidence now available for prescience on the part of numerous persons is quite impressive. It is not uncommon for a person to have a clear certainty of a specific event happening in the foreseeable future, and then have that actually happen just as the person had perceived it. Some occurrences of prescience take the form of information perceived in a numinous dream, some as a haunting awareness that draws itself over a person's consciousness and others as a sudden insight or awareness that then transpires, within a time frame that associates it inescapably with that previous moment of prescient knowing.

If such events of intuition, ESP, and prescience took place only in the lives of psychotic patients with confirmed diagnoses, we would not very likely accord them any further attention. We would assume that they were manifestations and symptoms of the psychosis. However, these are not the type of paranormal experiences that typically occur only in psychotic or schizophrenic patients. They occur consistently in stable and healthy persons and in many cases enhance their health and sense of wellbeing.

Another of the most pronounced and most researched forms of paranormal experience, on which a preliminary literature has already been developed, is that of near death experiences, particularly as reported so extensively by Moody and others.

NEAR DEATH EXPERIENCES AS PARANORMAL PHENOMENA

I have alluded to the fact that the veil separating time from eternity, the mundane from the transcendental, and the material from the spiritual, may well be thinner and more permeable than we generally think. It is not surprising that we believe it to be thick and impenetrable, since we do not experience very clearly the flow of insights or communication from one realm to the other. However, narratives of surprising moments, when that veil was opened briefly, have been reported ever since humans began to keep track of such things. Moreover, many of us have had such experience in one form or another, such as my own illumination by the divine spirit at age seven, described above.

Apparently the reason we are not more aware of the communication flow through the veil between the world of life and the afterlife, or between the mundane and transcendent worlds lies in the fact that the human experiences of such moments have been readily discounted as impossible, improbable, strange, or downright dangerous or crazy. That arms-length distancing from the paranormal, at least; and the categorical denial of the very existence of the paranormal, at most, has been especially prominent in the western world since the flowering of scientific research in the seventeenth and eighteenth centuries, as I noted above.

Our need to deal honestly with these psychospiritual realities, together with their long-standing presence in human experience and in the human record, can be discounted only at significant cost to us. The price we pay for such closed-mindedness is that we will fail to come to terms with a comprehensive understanding of the nature of our own selves, and of the psychospiritual potentials of human persons and community. Wherever the flavor of truth and reality can be savored, we should develop a lively appetite for it, and drink from those wells of wisdom to the extent that they will offer refreshing insight and knowledge.

My grandmother died in her late eighties. Her husband, my grandfather, died a number of years before her. They had been married for nearly seventy years, and had been the parents of fifteen children, fourteen of whom survived childhood and lived long lives. Because of the nature of this large immigrant family, my grandmother always referred to her husband as "Pa" and he referred to her as "Ma." I never remember hearing them use each others given names.

Grandmother was her vibrant, jovial, and warmhearted self until the last months of her life. During the last six weeks or so she was mainly in a coma in a nursing home. The day came when it seemed certain that she would die. Her large family gathered round in her room. As is frequently the case with coma victims, at the very end she suddenly awakened and became her old self again for a half hour or so. She conversed with her children, now growing old themselves. She expressed her love and warmth, and shared her typical humor about the situation.

Her conversation was lively to the very last. While busy talking, she suddenly stopped in mid-sentence, gazed upward toward her right, leaned forward, then with an indescribable look of joy on her face she reached out her hand, and called out, "Oh, Pa!" and in that moment she was gone. Obviously, in her moment of transition from time to eternity, she saw my grandfather who had come to receive her into the transcendent world. If that were a singular or unique event, we would find it difficult to comment upon it. Even then, we could not discount out of hand its empirical reality. However, a physician, Raymond A. Moody, Jr., has published an entire volume of reports of such experiences people have had at the threshold of death, the access point to eternity.[1]

Of course, there are those who discount such visionary events as the side effects of what happens to brain chemistry as the organism of a persons material self begins to shut down and mental operations close themselves out. It is my personal conviction that proposing such a hypothesis is quite unscientific, particularly without any demonstrable

---

1. Raymond A. Moody, Jr., *Life After Life* (New York: Bantam, 1976). First published in 1975, 35 printings by 1981.

proof. Sometimes, as Freud is reported to have declared, a cigar is just a cigar. The hypothesis that such an event is pretty much what it looks like should be given at least as much credence as the reductionist hypotheses of materialistic empirical science, which may wish, sometimes, to rule out notions of the ethereal spiritual operations in a human being, but is finding it increasingly impossible to do so in face of the mounting evidence.

Moody's work, together with numerous others which have flowed from his hypothesis, also cites a surprising body of evidence for "near death experiences" which cannot honestly be set aside without thoughtful analysis. Moreover, the evidence has a couple of facets which add greatly to its warrantability. First, the near death experiences cited by Moody, and in the testimony from numerous other sources, are largely the same kind of experiences in every case, though taking place in a great variety of circumstances. Secondly, these psychospiritual or ethereal events have a number of internal components, most of which are shared by all the near death experiences, cross-culturally and regardless of the nature of the person involved. On the face of it, there seems to be a substantial replication of the tangible experiences reported.

My grandmother's experience typifies one sort of near death experience, namely, that in which the person experiencing it actually dies and does not recover from that experience; but provides evidence of the death experience while it is happening. The more typical experience reported in the data is that of persons who have experienced some form of traumatic near death experience, from which they have returned to life. Of course, the reason for this latter form of near death experience appearing more prominently in the literature lies in the fact that those who experience the former type of such an event, as my grandmother did, are not able to tell their whole story. Those who return from a death or near death experience are able to report it. Most of the literature reporting these experiences is made up of collections of such case histories.

In her introduction to Moody's volume, Elizabeth Kubler-Ross, also a physician observes that it "is evident from his findings that the dying patient continues to have a conscious awareness of his environment after being pronounced clinically dead." She asserts that this is the same result that her own research in this area produced. Both her research and that of Moody "used the accounts of patients who have died and made a comeback, totally against . . . expectations, and often to the surprise of some highly sophisticated, well-known and certainly accomplished physicians."

The reports of this phenomenon are consistent in describing the experiences of the patients involved. All the patients indicate that they experienced a floating out of their bodies, and a feeling of an enormous sense of peace and wholeness. In this ethereal state, the near death experience included encounter with another ethereal person who appeared to assist them "in their transition to another level of existence." As in the case of my grandmother, "most were greeted by loved ones who had died before them, or by a religious figure who was significant in their life" and was congruent with their faith perspective.

Moody noted in the introduction to his book that his hope was that it would "draw attention to a phenomenon which is at once very widespread and very well-hidden ...."[2] Moody reported on 150 cases of persons who had experienced what they and/or their physicians described as death, but who either reported their experiences while dying or returned from that state and recovered. Their reports of the experiences were, of course, remarkable. Moody organized them into three categories in his attempt to subject them to scientific scrutiny and analysis.

The first type of event was that of "persons who were resuscitated after having been thought, adjudged, or pronounced clinically dead by their doctors." The second type was that of persons who, in the course of severe trauma or illness "came very close to physical death." The third was that of persons who died, and while they were dying they told their experiences to other people who were present and who later reported the story for posterity.[3] Moody decided in the end not to include in his book the data on the third category, since this was a secondhand report, at best, and there was, probably for that reason, less consistency in that set of data than in the other two categories. His book, therefore, treats the cases in which a person died, and returned from that state to report the experience personally. Then Moody focused his work on a further, in-depth analysis of the fifty prominent cases which typified the patterns in the entire set from the first two categories.

Moody found that the similarity of the various reports is so great and consistent that "one can easily pick out about fifteen separate elements which recur" repeatedly in the stories.[4] His description of the paradigmatic or typical story is as follows.

2. Moody, Op. Cit., 5.
3. Moody, Op. Cit., 16.
4. Ibid., 21.

> A man is dying and, as he reaches the point of greatest physical distress, he hears himself pronounced dead by his doctor. He begins to hear an uncomfortable noise, a loud ringing or buzzing, and at the same time feels himself moving very rapidly through a long dark tunnel. After this, he suddenly finds himself outside of his own physical body, but still in the immediate physical environment, and he sees his own body from a distance, as though he is a spectator. He watches the resuscitation attempt from this unusual vantage point and is in a state of emotional upheaval.

After a while, he collects himself and becomes more accustomed to his odd condition. He notices that he still has a "body," but one of a very different nature and with very different powers from the physical body he has left behind. Soon other things begin to happen. Others come to meet and to help him. He glimpses the spirits of relatives and friends who have already died, and a loving warm spirit of a kind he has never encountered before—a being of light—appears before him. This being asks him a question, nonverbally, to make him evaluate his life and helps him along by showing him a panoramic, instantaneous playback of the major events of his life. At some point he finds himself approaching some sort of barrier or border, apparently representing the limit between earthly life and the next life. Yet he finds that he must go back to the earth, that the time for his death has not yet come. At this point he resists, for by now he is taken up with his experiences in the afterlife and does not want to return. He is overwhelmed by intense feelings of joy, love, and peace. Despite his attitude, though, he somehow reunites with his physical body and lives.

Later he tries to tell others, but he has trouble doing so. In the first place, he can find no human words adequate to describe these unearthly episodes. He also finds that others scoff, so he stops telling other people. Still the experience affects his life profoundly, especially his views about death and its relationship to life.[5]

This is a composite model of all the stories reported by Moody. Each element was present in numerous stories. None were present in all. Most were present in most of the stories. The longer the person was in the state of having been pronounced dead, the deeper into the experience described in the model he or she reports to have gotten. Moreover, the deeper the experience was the more detailed, complete, and colorful the

---

5. Moody, Op. Cit., 21–23.

person's report of it consistently proved to be. Each person had virtually the same difficulty describing the experience through which he or she had come. Their common testimony was that the words we generally use and the conceptual categories familiar to human discourse just do not provide useful resources of thought and language to describe adequately the death or near death experiences.

The remarkable uniformity of four or five categories of ethereal experience in Moody's case studies is particularly noteworthy. First of all, the experience in each case included being out of one's body and viewing the scene from afar as a spectator. This suggests that some ethereal aspect of the person involved was able to objectify the death experience as something happening "out there," so to speak, and separate from the essential self. It makes one immediately think of the reports in the gospels of Jesus appearances to his disciples and others after his death. It is clear in those stories that it was not the dead body from the cross and the tomb that the disciples were seeing. If it were it would have been easy immediately to recognize it, however, in none of the appearances did the humans recognize that it was Jesus until he did something to manifest himself to them.

Paul calls it Jesus' glorified body, like that which we shall all possess after death (I Cor. 15). Both Paul and Peter declare that Jesus died in the flesh and was resurrected in the spirit, as shall all of us one day according to their worldview. In any case, Jesus is reported, after his death, as coming and going without restrictions of time, space, or materiality. He could enter and leave rooms without opening windows or doors. He needed no material food, though he could ingest some food in order to demonstrate to his disciples that he was real and not just a figment of their hysterical imaginations.

Similarly, persons who describe their death experiences say that they were able to see their own bodies lying in some place external to their real selves. Their reports indicate that there was a certain singular quality of relief, freedom, joy, consolation, and pleasure associated with their release from their material bodies. Most of them resisted any return to their bodies, though that was required in every case, of course, for the person to return to this state of mundane material life.

A second common element of note is the fact that in each case the "dead" persons found themselves in a tunnel or narrow valley which led to some unknown destiny. The similarity and variety of this element are both interesting. The similarity lies in the fact that in every case the person faced a journey through a narrow way, through or beyond a barrier, and into a place unknown. The variety of characteristics of this valley or tunnel included the fact that some persons experienced the tunnel as filled with light, some found it dark, some found the valley mysterious and awesome, some found it pleasant and inviting.

Virtually all the persons experienced a third feature of the event, namely, a dramatic and unusual kind of sound, accompanying them in the valley or tunnel. Here again the variety is interesting. Some heard a repetitious beating sound, something like the rhythm of a heart beat, or a train passing over the joints in the trestle. Many heard music, sometimes somber and ominous, sometimes like the joyful ringing of bells.

The fourth aspect worth noting, especially, was the almost universal experience, in these cases, of a person or a number of persons coming from "the other side," so to speak, to meet the "dying or dead" person, for the purpose of protecting, assisting, or guiding him or her. Such persons were always people who had died sometime before and who were familiar to the "newly dead" person. Usually they were loved ones.

Moody reported that in two cases the person telling the near death story indicated that a familiar and congenial person or voice came into the tunnel and instructed him or her to go back into his or her body, declaring that he or she was not yet dead and had further purposes to accomplish in life. The two cases in which this was explicit typified all the others in which something of this sort was implicit.

For good and obvious reasons, Moody drew his book to an end with explanations and impressions, not conclusions. He carefully analyzed supernatural explanations, natural explanations, and psychological explanations. Under natural explanations he explored how near death experiences might be induced by medications, or biochemistry changes, physiological changes and neurological or brain changes, associated with trauma. The psychological possibilities for explaining the near death experiences, such as dreams, hallucinations, and delusions, were also carefully studied. None of these options, for a variety of solid reasons, could account for the nature, consistency, frequency, and uniformity of the reports of near death phenomena.

A Gallup Poll, conducted in the early 1980s, indicated that over eight million Americans have had near death experiences.[6] Plato recounted a story of a soldier, named Er, who was injured in battle, along with numerous of his comrades. The bodies lay for ten days on the battlefield before relatives could come to reclaim them. When they arrived they were surprised that the bodies were all badly decayed except for the body of Er. He was carried home and placed upon the funeral pyre, at which point he revived, stood up, and recounted what he had learned while "on the other side."[7]

The story of Er reminds one of the strange events associated with the death of Alexander the Great. He was declared dead and so his generals divided up the empire. Ptolemy took his emperor's body and carried it to Egypt where he buried it in an alabaster tomb. The amazing thing, of course, was that Alexander's body did not decay for a long time after he was discerned to be dead. One wonders what sort of near death experience he might have reported to us, had he not been closed up in a box and trundled roughly in a primitive wagon over undeveloped terrain for a few weeks, from Babylon to Alexandria in Egypt.

Atwater indicates that he himself had a near death experience and was professionally interested in the residual effects of such experiences in the subsequent lives of those who had them. Not all such persons reported the positive and empowering processes that most of Moody's cases show. Atwater categorizes the near death events as positive and negative. In the positive category eight items are listed, mainly the same as in Moody's taxonomy. There we have the sensation of 1) floating out of one's body, 2) passing through a dark tunnel or black hole, 3) ascending toward a light at the end of the tunnel, 4) being greeted by and having conversation with friendly voices or people and feeling overwhelming acceptance and love, 5) seeing a panoramic review of one's life, 6) feeling a heavenly warmth and the reluctance to return to the mundane material world, 7) perceiving an altered sense of time and space with sensations of incomparable beauty, 8) feeling disappointment at being revived.

However, there are those reporting near death experiences that found it to be a wretched process of 1) seeing lifeless apparitions, 2) passing through barren or empty expanses, 3) enduring threats or

---

6. P. M. H. Atwater, *Coming Back to Life: The After-Effects of the Near-Death Experience* (New York: Ballantine, 1988) xiii and 2.

7. Atwater, Op. Cit., 5.

overwhelming silence, 4) perceiving danger and the threat of potential violence, 5) having a sense of hellish coldness and isolation. Persons who have had these negative experiences, of course, have no fond memories of the experience. They do not wish to return to the other side and want to stave off death as long as possible. Atwater reports persons who contemplated or attempted suicide, after a negative near death experience of some kind, lost all inclination toward self-termination.

On the other hand, Kubler-Ross, Moody, and Atwater all report that those who have survived near death as a positive experience might be considered in a certain sense, at least, to be non-survivors. That is, the residual effect is often a resistance to settle back down in the reality of this mundane material world, always longing to return to the sense of utter blessedness the near death experience meant for them. Not all, but many, apparently wish to return to the other side sooner rather than later. They feel that they are no longer really citizens of this world, but have entered into participation in another, more inviting state of life.

Atwater's personal experience with near death process was a positive one and the acclimatization to living life again in this present world required a major adjustment. That in turn required a conscious and intentional effort to find a way to integrate the meaning of the experience into the spiritual processes of daily life. In this quest, what proved to be of immense help was the liturgies of religious behavior and the effort to find at their center the spiritual wellspring which produced those liturgies, meanings, doctrines, and behaviors in the first place. This was an effort to recover the original spiritual experience of those persons from whose lives and spirits the forms and functions of those liturgies arose. Atwater makes a telling observation at this point, "Spirituality is based upon a personal, intimate experience of God. There are no standards or dogmas, only precedents; for individual knowing or gnosis is honored."[8]

Moody originally wrote his book on near death experiences in 1975, referring to 150 such events. He continued his research in this specific area and twenty years later he could testify to having studied 20,000 such reports. The most dramatic and most complete he had ever encountered, he stated, was that of Dannion Brinkley.[9] In 1974 Brinkley

---

8. Atwater, Op. Cit., 232.
9. Dannion Brinkley and Paul Perry, *Saved by the Light*, (New York: Random House, 1994).

was struck in the head by lightening while speaking on the telephone. Moody interviewed him in 1976. Brinkley's story seemed preposterous and Moody initially discounted it. His narrative included the typical out of body experience. He saw his dead body while leaving it and upon returning to it. He was also drawn along the usual journey. A tunnel came to him, so to speak, and in the process his dominant experience was that of moving toward a brilliant light. The encompassing beauty was marked by the singular "sounds of seven chimes ringing in rhythmic succession".[10]

Brinkley felt like an unencumbered spirit, with an infinite lightness of being. He seems to have achieved greater progress than the average person in near death experiences. He passed through the barrier to a spiritual realm where kind and powerful beings illumined him with a full review of his entire life and allowed him to assess his successes and failures. The review of his life carried him into deep experiences of guilt, shame, and grief; all of which the Being of Light brought to his consciousness and also gave him complete forgiveness and consolation.

Thereafter he found himself in a beautiful city of crystal and light where he "sat in the presence of thirteen Beings of Light who filled him with knowledge".[11] The spiritual beings imparted esoteric knowledge to him about the future. It was this element which eventually persuaded Moody of the authenticity of Brinkley's report and experience. In 1976, Brinkley indicated that the spiritual beings informed him that the Soviet Union would break up in 1989, that a Middle East war would take place in 1990 in the desert, in which a small country would invite a large country. "According to the Beings of Light, there would be a clashing of two armies one of which would be destroyed."[12]

For Brinkley, the residual effects of his death experience include an unprecedented persistent clairvoyance in which he can read minds, foresee things that will happen, know things about other persons' lives by ESP and intuition. That is, Brinkley's capacity for para-psychological ways of knowing seems to have been heightened, strengthened, expanded, and clarified. He was not aware of any of these capacities in himself prior to the near death event. His clairvoyance is focused mainly on be-

10. Moody, Op. Cit., 8
11. Moody, Op. Cit., x.
12. Ibid., xi.

ing able to predict the future and read the mind of anyone immediately upon encountering him or her.

It is mystifying as to why anyone who has had a near death experience should be able to exercise such clairvoyance. No one knows why that should be or why it is the case. However, Melvin Morse and Paul Perry, in *Transformed by the Light*, demonstrated from their research that people who have been through a near death process are three times as likely to experience verifiable and empirically measurable para-psychological events (ESP, prescience, intuition), as the average human being.[13]

The authors focus on qualitative assessments of the near death experiences. Their work is a rich and enriching review of the aspects typical in such events. They are particularly interested in the after-effects. Their model consequently resembles that of other such studies. Their findings include the following: feelings of peace (77%), out of body experiences (65%), brilliant light (72%), life review (17%), unearthly realm (24%), tunnel (51%), feelings of joy (31%), ESP (33%), and visions of the future (13%). Among those with visions of the future, the visions referred to the world's future (22%), to the person's own future (48%), or to both (29%). Approximately 72% experienced some change in their nature or feeling world after their recovery from the near death event. Particular changes included changes in attitude toward death (82%), conviction of survival of bodily death (48%), becoming more spiritual (42%), becoming more socially conscious (40%), and becoming a better friend and person (90%).

Morse and Perry expanded their research to include the near death experiences of children and found that the data is essentially the same as that in adults. They published the results on children in *Closer to the Light, Learning From the Near-Death Experiences of Children*.[14]

The works of Michael Newton regarding near death experiences and spirituality have very recently become the most popular in the field. He is considered by some to be the current dean of this research and its interpretation. He is a licensed counselor and a certified hypnotherapist. He is interested in assisting people with behavior modification and accessing their spiritually central selves. His *Journey of Souls, Case Studies*

---

13. Melvin Morse and Paul Perry, *Transformed by The Light, The Powerful Effects of Near-Death Experiences on People's Lives* (New York: Parapsychology Press, 1996).

14. Melvin Morse and Paul Perry, *Closer to the Light, Learning From the Near-Death Experiences of Children* (New York: Villard, 1990).

of Life Between Lives is a most gratifying read and confirms all of the foregoing.[15] While his concept of spirituality derives more from Eastern Religions and New Age Thinking than from the three Abrahamic Faiths (Christianity, Judaism, and Islam), there is much in his ruminations and research from which anyone can learn regarding the nature of our authenticity as spiritual beings potentially in touch with the divine spirit.

In this regard it is of value to share some observations by Morton T. Kelsey on para-psychological ways of knowing and their relationship to spirituality. He wrote many books related to this question, but two of them are of particular note. One is *God, Dreams, and Revelation*, in which he takes standard dream interpretation theory from Freud to the end of the 20th century and demonstrates that it is an empowering enhancement of our understanding of spiritual experience that humans have been dealing with throughout human history. He elaborates the fact, moreover, that this psychological process is also a spiritual process and relates directly to much of the biblical message on spirituality, revelation, intimations from God's spirit, and growth in our openness to that divine spirit communicating with our own.

His other relevant book is *The Christian and the Supernatural*. He makes a considerable point of the fact that if we are not open to the empirical reality of ESP, prescience, and intuition as legitimate and normal forms of para-psychological knowing, we miss a vast field of data and experience which is enmeshed with our spiritual vitality and with biblical teaching. Kelsey's central point is one I endorse enthusiastically and this present volume assumes it as a fundamental underpinning of my entire argument. That central point is that the world is replete with the pervasive presence of God's spirit in all forms of life and existence. That spirit functions in every aspect of human life and experience, and is perpetually endeavoring to access the communication lines with our spirits.

In that enterprise the divine spirit is capable of employing any and every potential of human experience as a channel for intimating to us the meanings and consolations of God's presence and grace. If we close ourselves off to the potentials of the para-psychological, we repress a special aspect of the God-given paranormal right brain function, so as to limit ourselves to the rational and empirical. We foreclose a vast domain of potential encounter between God's spirit and our own. Our best

---

15. Michael Newton, *Journey of Souls, Case Studies of Life Between Lives* (St. Paul: Llewellyn Publications, 2002).

option, instead, is to open ourselves to God's spirit in whatever form it may choose to come to us, by whatever channel it may employ, and so live the life of the spirit more intentionally, consciously, expectantly, and hopefully.

The divine spirit can speak to us in ESP, intuition, prescience, rational thought, near death experiences, empirical science, heuristic analysis, written books, worship liturgies, and phenomenological investigation. All truth is God's truth, wherever we find it and from whatever source. If we find it in the Bible or another Sacred Scripture, it probably makes sense to call it a special revelation. If we find in nature, science, or our own paranormal or mystical experiences, we may do well to recognize that such revelations appear to be natural and common.

Undoubtedly Ken R. Vincent is correct in his epilogue to *Visions of God, from the Near Death Experience*.[16]

> The Spirit of God is over all the earth, and in all things;
> It is in God that we live and breathe and have our being.
> All that is is God,
> And while we are here
> There is only one rule:
> Never hurt anyone,
> And there is only one commandment:
> Love one another.[17]

---

16. Ken R. Vincent, *Visions of God from the Near Death Experience* (Burdett, New York: Larson Publications, 1994).

17. Some of the argument in this section appeared in a substantially different form in J. Harold Ellens (2008), *Understanding Religious Experiences, What the Bible Says About Spirituality*, Westport, CT: Praeger; and is used here with permission.

4

The View from the Bridge

My mother's death proved quite unexpectedly to be an intense paranormal experience for me. Mother died at 90 years of age, after some time abed with a broken spine, incurred in a fall from tripping on a carpet, so unfortunately typical of the elderly. Born in February of 1904, death sought her out on the night my parents completed 70 years of marriage in March of 1994. She was a spirited lady of infinite grace, until she was reduced to bed by her injury. Even then, she lived out those quiet days "on the shelf," so to speak, with a peaceful and patient spirit.

My wife, Mary Jo, and I were attending the annual convention of the Christian Association for Psychological Study in San Antonio, Texas. That city and region are a particularly delightful part of Texas. For us it was a very special time because I had been assigned to Fort Sam Houston and to the General Staff of the Health Services Command for many years during my tenure as an army Colonel. There were a lot of familiar places and delightful haunts we enjoyed revisiting, and there is always the river walk which the city continues to improve and extend. San Antonio is a place to spend some pleasant leisure time.

That year was the fifth anniversary of my having turned over the reigns, after fifteen years as executive director of CAPS, so the program planners celebrated me with a roast. We all had a great deal of fun. However, in the early morning of the third day I was suddenly struck with an overwhelming sense of doom. A great heaviness, lethargy, burdensomeness, and pathos came over me. It was wholly uncharacteristic of me. I mentioned to Mary Jo that I just could not explain my feelings but that it was possible that I was actually experiencing the preliminary processes of dying. It felt very much like that. After my second heart attack, I had undergone major heart surgery two years earlier, and I had reason to know what I was talking about. I was almost aphasic, immobile, without affect, and so oppressed I found it difficult to breath. We had visited a lovely retirement center for military officers at breakfast at 7:30, and had enjoyed the experience sufficiently that we considered acquiring a condominium there. As we were preparing to return to the convention hotel I was suddenly struck down with the overwhelming sense that death was upon me.

When we returned to the hotel the sense of doom persisted and progressively increased. When we arrived at the hotel at around noon, we were met in the lobby by the manager and the director of CAPS. I was informed that I urgently needed to telephone my office. When I did so, I was informed that my mother had been suffering heart failure that morning and had died just before my return call. I prepared immediately to return home.

My mother and I had a close emotional attachment from my earliest memories forward. Because of her frequent illnesses during my childhood, I always longed for a more intense relationship with her than was possible. Because of the trauma of Esther's death in my sixth year of life, I was an insecure and neurotic child and an awkward adolescent, seriously lacking in self-confidence and self-esteem. My mother's warmth and encouragement to me, combined with my sense of precarious neediness, formed more co-dependence than was good for me. As a result, appropriate disengagement from her at the end of my adolescence was less complete than it is supposed to be. Departure for college at age 17, followed by years of military duty thereafter separated me from her rather brutally and permanently. Consequently, there was a lot of unresolved individuation process that marked my life until well into my middle years.

That seems to me now to have some bearing on the nature of my subconscious connectedness to her. What strikes me about the events of that March day in 1994 is the fact that when she lay dying, without my knowledge and with no one expecting it then, at some level of awareness I experienced the process of her dying, and the anguish of having her torn away from me. Something in me was aware of her dying, and something in me died with her. I do not know, of course, whether my anguish was mainly unconscious grief over losing her; or a literal sharing in the ordeal of her death in some way, while she was experiencing it; or the pain of having her torn away from me in some final way.

The point that is clear to me is that I was personally participating in her experience of the process of dying and it felt like the experience of dying in me. Without any clear clue to what was happening, without any warning or supposition that she was near death, and without any information of her dying process, ESP transmitted the experience of her dying across the space of 1500 miles as she was in the process of experiencing it herself. Psychospiritually she and I experienced it together though we were remarkably remote from one another. The power of the intimations and communications of the spirit force in us is infinitely beyond description, but profoundly real.

I have a scholarly acquaintance who reports a very similar event in his life. Russ Llewellyn tells his story like this. He says that one day when he was a young psychologist he visited the farm where his mother grew up and where her mother had died. While there he decided to walk out behind the homestead and up a hill on which stood the country church and its typical graveyard. As he ascended the hill he was progressively overcome with a deep sadness for which he could not discern the source.

> So I stopped and asked myself where it was coming from. Was it from me because of childhood nostalgia, having played and fished for crawdads in the creek below and having visited the farm during summers as a child? No. Was it about me from some other source? No. Was it feelings I was having for my mother? No. Was it feelings I was aware of which were my mother's feelings? Yes. That was it! Years later, I relayed this story to my mother who began to cry and said that she knew what it was. Because of her mother's sudden death after her senior year in high school, and her mother's burial in the cemetery at the church on the hill top, my mother said that she never crossed the gate into the cemetery again during all the times she went to church. It became clear as my mother talked that her trauma became symbolized by the cemetery and the gate became a phobic object. Crossing it would open the door to her pain. That is what my story opened to her. I realized it was not my feelings I was aware of, but my mother's that overcame me. I was not feeling for my mother, nor having empathic feelings for my mother. I was suffering her pain.[1]

---

1. Russ Llewellyn, Religious and Spiritual Miracle Events in Real-Life Experiences, Vol. 1, *Religious and Spiritual Events*, Ch 14 in J. Harold Ellens, *Miracles: God, Science, and Psychology in the Paranormal*, 3 vols. (Westport, CT: Praeger, 2008), 251.

Llewellyn believes that this was a moment of the spirit that opened in him the ability to feel the emotional pain of others, whether they are consciously or unconsciously trying to hide it; or are open to expressing it. He declares that this is a gift of the spirit that is beyond empathy. It has greatly enhanced his therapeutic practice and his life. Obviously, living life close to the wind of the spirit opens us to the potential of living close to the spirits of those around us.

When I conduct funerals I am often aware of this experience of my mother's death. It plays out the backdrop to what I am led to say in funeral homilies. It reminds me that the material world and the spiritual world are separated, if at all, by a highly permeable screen. Communication back and forth through that thin veil is much more frequent and lively than we generally assume. It usually seems to me, as we are gathered for the farewell ceremonies of departed loved ones, that the last act of the deceased, so to speak, has been to invite us to that special place of contemplation; to that rare opportunity of envisioning for a little while the nature of our lives viewed in the light of eternity, or of eternity viewed in terms of the experiences of our practical daily lives.

Ian Baker, an eastern contemplative, stated succinctly an important insight that we western positivists may need to learn, namely, "to recognize that there are no inherent boundaries between external reality and the circuitry of consciousness."[2] Baker thinks that unanticipated spiritual treasures are revealed to us when a juxtaposition occurs of some external event and our inner spiritual openness to its meaning for us personally. This opens the subtle channels "through which ordinary perception transforms into revelation, receiving through surrender" to the experience what lies beyond what the mind can ever grasp. "In an unimpeded flow of energies larger than self or other, doors open into the hidden lands of the heart that . . . exist only in potential until realized in the fullest, fearless, unbounded expanse of one's innermost being, beyond the productions of intellect or faith or divisions between what's external and what's internal. In the full openness of the unknown there are neither curtains nor doors . . ."[3]

Few have expressed more articulately what I have experienced in paranormal events like that which engaged me in sharing my mother's

---

2. Ian Baker, *A Journey into the Last Secret Place, The Heart of the World*, New York: Penguin Press, (2004), 295.

3. Ibid, 290.

death ordeal, and like those which were clearly sudden, life embracing, moments of divine illumination—conjoining of my spirit with the spirit of God that I believe is rampant in the universe. Baker, it seems to me, has caught at the flood the authentic intimations of this long repressed world of transcendent reality that we generally miss, though it is pervasive in our daily mundane pilgrimage. It awaits us all just behind the materiality of our daily lives. It waits for those who have the eyes to see and ears to hear.

The death of loved ones, and the funerals to celebrate their living and dying, is like an invitation to stand for a little while on the bridge between life and death, here and there, now and then, between time and eternity. It is important, whenever we get a chance in life, to view our world from the middle of that bridge. I have three sons and four daughters. All of them have always been as fascinated with bridges as have I. They find them as exciting, enjoyable, and revealing as I do. Whether it is just a log thrown across a woodland stream, or what in Michigan we call the Big Bridge, the Mackinac, bridges are vastly fascinating. You can get a view from a bridge that you cannot get from any other perspective in life. To stand at the middle of a bridge and have a careful look at your world from there makes life look altogether different than does any other experience. It is inevitably a remarkable revelation; and it is wholly unforgettable.

I was first struck by the wonder of bridges, and the illumination they can afford us, when my high school graduation trip took us into the wilds of the Upper Peninsula of Michigan to visit the Tahquamenon Falls. I suppose such a trip does not sound like much to the youth who these days travel to exotic tropical places or even overseas, on such occasions. However, in 1949 such an adventure into the woods and river basins of the wild country of the natural world and wilderness of our state actually really felt like a journey to the ends of the earth. In the first place, we needed to travel by bus into those northern climes; and then transfer to a narrow gauge logging train that carried us endless miles through birch and maple forests very similar to those I later traversed in the vast expanses of Soviet Siberia.

Finally, near the end of the day, we arrived at the river edge. There a surprisingly large river steamer was tied up to a rough hewn pier. We boarded the ship and settled in for dinner and a night's rest, anticipating our departure down stream at first light. The next morning when I entered the dining room for breakfast, we had already loosed our moorings and entered the main stream of that large, impressive river. I stood at the prow for most of the day-long voyage to the falls. I simply could not believe what life looked like from the middle of the stream as we wound our way along the curves and twists of the Tahquamenon. The gorge itself was infinitely interesting and colorful, cut through the geological layers formed by millions of years of creation; and every few minutes was a new serendipitous repetition of surprises. Every turn in the river was a new revelation, filling my whole self with wonder and elation. I felt a kind of transcendence. It was the view from the bridge that did it; in this case the bridge of the steamer. It was a harbinger of later experiences that awaited me, such as the now more common view from the massive Mackinac. That trip on the Tahquamenon changed my life. I could never look at things the same again.

I have crossed many bridges since that day. Since then, however, I have never been able to cross a bridge just to rush to the other side. There are two ways to cross a bridge. It can be just another incident in a journey to somewhere else, or it can be an objective in itself, a moment to stop and look, and listen; to get the view from the middle of the bridge that can change one's life. It can be a season of contemplation, meaning, and revelation. Some people cross bridges just to get somewhere else on their hurried travail of life. Others cross bridges to savor the flavor of life's travail from one meaningful moment to another; moments to reflect on one's place in time and under pressure of eternity, moments before the face of God and looking for God's spirit.

Trying to get a view from the middle of the river has persisted as an intense desire for me whenever possible. I have crossed the long, high Mackinac Bridge frequently, the Golden Gate and Oakland Bay Bridges, and all the wonderful bridges of New York: the George Washington Bridge, the Brooklyn Bridge, the Verrazano, and the Tappan Zee. I crossed the bridges of the Rhine at Remagen, Mainz, Worms, and Cologne; of the Danube at Vienna and Budapest, of the Arno in Florence, the Elbe, the Don, and the Nile. Often I feel rushed along by the traffic, too hurried by the pressure of others to get a proper view from that bridge for myself. I want a time to stop my journey, hold it in suspension, to get off the speeding train of life, so to speak, and hold in quiet, reflective contemplation that view from the middle of the bridge. I hunger for it. I need it at some deep center point in myself.

It is very important to get the view from the bridge. We need those moments when we are forced to stand on that bridge between life and death, compelled to view ourselves and our times in that light of eternity which shines through the screen when we celebrate the passing of one we love or esteem. Conversely, it is a critical necessity to stand in the middle of the bridge and contemplate eternity in the light of our personal daily lives. I will eventually be buried in Arlington Cemetery. I often go there when in Washington to view its august aesthetics and its somber symbols. My late brother was the Sergeant of the Guard at the Tomb of the Unknown Soldiers for four years of his military duty. The place holds inexpressible depth and scope of meaning and of vision and illumination for me as an old soldier, and as a retired Army Chaplain who laid so many of those courageous men to rest. My mother's death drew me more profoundly to that place of vision and illumination than any other death in my life so far. It was a paranormal experience in which I was psychospiritually drawn into the very process and the travail of her own dying.

What awesome reality is it that reaches across 1500 miles of space and embraces two persons dear to one another and connects them at the soul? What is it that affords a mutuality of supportive presence in those moments of extremity? Some major dynamic of profound meaning is at work, and we should find out more about that if we really want to understand the mystery of our psychospiritual lives and our life in the divine spirit. Is that profound set of forces merely an extension of our ordinary psychic life, or is it a touch of heaven and of God? I should like to know. We should try to figure it out carefully, honestly, and scientifically. If it is a special connection with the spirit of God, life is a remarkably different kind of thing, going on in a remarkably different kind of spiritual matrix, than most people think. In any case, there is nothing so revealing about the nature and meaning of life, as a sustained view from the bridge between us and the eternal.

Undoubtedly, Ian Baker is correct in suggesting that the boundaries we assume, and in terms of which we operate our lives, are projections of our way of thinking and imagining reality. In point of fact, there seems to be increasing evidence that there are no impervious boundaries between our spirits, which inherently or inevitably impede our potential for mutuality, for connection, for communication. Neither time nor space nor materiality are real boundaries between us and others, or between our mundane existence and our spiritual transcendence. The boundaries between earth and heaven, time and eternity, are more imagined than real. The screen is permanently permeable. God's spirit operates in heaven and earth as though the boundary and screen do not exist—or in any case do not have the form of the barriers that we usually think they are. The problem is not barriers between us, and between us and the divine spirit. The problem is that we have lost our skill in using and trusting our paranormal capacities for knowing reality.

5

Sailing Close to the Wind

I AM NOT MUCH of a sailor. I do not really like boats and water very much. I have a friend who regularly invites me to sail with him on his large sailboat. It has a number of sails and also a huge and powerful Chrysler inboard engine, to help with getting in and out of the harbor, as well as with occasions of emergency or dead calm. He sails it across Lake St. Clair over to Canada and back. He really gets a lot of joy out of that. I do not enjoy it much. I would rather be at home reading a good book or tramping through the forest with my son.

However, there is one form of sailing I really like. That is sailing a small boat like a sun fish or sail fish, preferably alone with the wind and the waves, and the sun. Alone in such a small boat is incredibly exciting, since it puts one completely at the mercy of nature and one's own skill in managing the wind and water. It is an experience of deep saturation in the raw forces of nature. It is intensely sensuous and spiritual.

I have discovered something about sailing such a small boat that is a metaphor for my life—indeed, for all human life. If you wish to get the full benefit out of the experience and get where you are going, it is crucial that you sail close to the wind. Of course, you can simply fall before the wind, but then it takes you wherever it wants to take you. The wind blows where it will. You hear the sound of it. You see the effects of it, but you do not know where it is coming from or where it will blow you. Simply falling before the wind, letting out your mainsail and jib, will give you a thrilling fast ride to nowhere. But if you want to get where you are going you need to sail close to the wind, rather than just falling before it.

Sailing close to the wind means that you head the boat into the wind at as sharp and angle to the wind as possible. Then you have maximum control over where the boat goes. You can even sail into the wind in that way, zigzagging slightly, so as to take full advantage of the wind sliding right off your sail and forcing you along almost exactly in the direction from which the wind it coming. Tacking into the wind can take you exactly where you need to go, indeed, in quite a different direction from falling before the wind. Then you can get where you are going; and the experience of sailing into the wind is exciting, challenging, requires you to keep alert to how the wind is blowing, and being completely open to letting the wind do your work for you.

In the nearly eight decades of my life, I have experienced a surprising number of life-changing paranormal events. I have noticed in this process that to be alert to these experiences for what they are, and to acquire from them the constructive life-changing impact that they can convey, it helps a great deal to be living one's life close to the wind of the spirit. That is, living life facing into the wind, holding yourself thoroughly open to the breath of the spirit, and letting the force of the wind of the spirit take you to your destiny.

The Bible has a lot to say about living in terms of the divine spirit. It identifies a lot of people who did so and tells their stories for our edification. The Bible speaks frequently of persons who were known as Seers or prophets. These were persons of a high level of spiritual intuition and fervency, who frequently spoke as though their insights were given them from some transcendent authority. They were quite sure that the source was the Holy Spirit of God. They were men and women who lived life close to the wind of the divine spirit blowing in this world of human experience.

However, the Bible struggled with the problem of sorting out which of these were authentic Seers, true or false prophets. It was important to be able to discern which of their messages were true and which false. In the end the judgment usually turned on whether the prophecy came true or the vision of the Seer proved useful and constructive. The main function of these visionaries, however, was not to predict the future but to make divine claims regarding the meaning of a current situation. The Seer or prophet functioned as a person who was bright and inspired enough and informed enough to rise above the ordinary parochial perspective and interpret the local events of history and life in terms of "the big picture," so to speak.

Among the prophets of Israel whose prophecies are preserved in the Bible, for example, we have a rather long list of what are know as the Ethical Prophets. Their work does not involve much prediction of the future. It has to do, instead, with announcing God's ethical claims upon the life and behavior of the Israelite nations, right then and there. They had two objectives, neither of which was magical. They intended to declare that bad behavior was bad and the people ought to quit it, and that behavior has consequences. They were Ethical Prophets, not predictors of the future. They said, "Woe to those who call evil good."

When a visionary was a person who lived a spiritual life of intense discernment of the presence of God in the world, and of the intimations of the divine spirit in his or her personal quest, he or she was usually able to inform the community of behavior, or courses of action, that seemed in line with and appropriate to God's will in this world. Frequently, such a highly developed spiritual person, living life close to the wind, could also see what the future course and consequences of present behavior or communal actions were likely to be. In that sense, the visionary, Seer, or prophet could foresee the future with its potential for prosperity or pain. Undoubtedly, there were also moments in ancient times, as there are in our present day, when such visionary folks were so in tune with the divine spirit present in the world everywhere, that they intuited intimations from God's spirit in their own spirits. They experienced bold visions like Abraham's theophany that God is a God of grace (Gen 12, 17); and not a God of threat who solves all his ultimate problems by a quick resort to ultimate violence, as most people thought in those days.

This posture, of living life close to the wind of the spirit, was never limited to the biblical narratives, history, community, or era. In every age and community there have been those identified personages who were sources of divine wisdom. While I was a college student, Professor Harry Jellema, of towering fame in our community, was noted for incredibly creative ways of getting at knotty intellectual and scientific problems. As I have mentioned in earlier chapters, I once heard him ruminating about where the insights he had came from. He was sure they were the direct gift of God's spirit. There is no difference between this claim, universal among the prophetic figures in the history of religion and spirituality of all ages and communities, and the similar claims of intimations from the divine spirit, experienced and testified by key figures in the Bible.

It is not easy to discern the difference, as visionaries, between Samuel, Isaiah, Ezekiel, John, Paul, Edgar Casey, Harry Jellema, Deepak Chopra, Colin Powell, and similar popular figures of the last or present century. Most likely there is no need to try to do so. The objective is to discern what is paradigmatic in the nature and function of such persons, true visionaries who live or lived with their spiritual sail set close to the wind of the divine urges in this world everywhere. We need to know how that works.

Biblical forms of spirituality all relate in the final analysis to the role of the prophetic visionary. In I Samuel 9:9 there is something of a definition of this kind of person. There we read that in early Israelite history, when someone wished to inquire of God about anything, he or she sought out a Seer "for he who is now called a prophet was formerly called a Seer." He was acknowledged as the person who lived intimately with God, was open to the intimations of God's spirit, and performed the religious rites which symbolized the common people's relationship with God and God's with them. There was something discernable about the Seer that made it clear that he searched for God, walked with God, talked with God, had epiphanies of God's presence, counted on God, and celebrated God's presence. Therefore, the people found it natural to expect that he talked *for* God, as well. When his visions proved useful and healing, and his prognostications regarding the future came true, his authority and credentials were confirmed.

We easily shelve those stories from the Bible into a special niche of supernatural claims and so rule out their genuine authenticity as well as rid ourselves of the notion that the same kind of thing could still be happening in our day, and could happen in our lives. That would be completely erroneous. There was nothing more supernatural about the visions or experiences with the divine spirit in biblical times than in our own times. The operations of the spirit are the same now as then. The experience of human illumination by the divine spirit were as paranormal then as now, except that then they were recognized as intimations and manifestations of the spirit, and in our scientific age we have more difficulty taking that fact for granted, as they did. Nonetheless, these very paranormal events have continued to happen throughout history and happen constantly today.

There are numerous passages in the Bible, among the reports on David and his kingdom, which indicate that on David's royal staff was a Seer named Gad. He came to David regularly to inform him of some problem in a course of action that David or the people of Israel were undertaking. Three Seers who were associated with David are reported to have written books, but apparently none of them have survived, unfortunately. In I Chronicles 29:26-30 we are informed:

> David the son of Jesse reigned over all Israel. The time that he reigned over Israel was forty years; he reigned seven years in Hebron, and thirty three years in Jerusalem. Then he died in a good old age, full of days, riches, and honor; and Solomon his son reigned in his stead. Now the acts of King David, from the first to last, are written in the Chronicles of Samuel the seer, and in the Chronicles of Nathan the prophet, and in the Chronicles of Gad the seer, with accounts of all his rule and his might and of the circumstances that came upon him and upon Israel, and upon all the kingdoms of the countries.

Implied in this account is the fact that these Seers were learned men who were literate and produced literature. Apparently, therefore, the society of the time was well educated and operated with a significant sense of the presence of God; and of human capacities to experience that presence and discern what intimations the divine spirit regularly intended to provide humans. A similar epitaph is written for Solomon in II Chronicles 9:29-31, and for his son, Rehoboam, in II Chronicles 12:13-16, confirming essentially the same state of affairs. Visionaries who lived life close to the wind of the spirit, such as Nathan, Iddo, Ahijah, and Shemaiah served these kings with divine instruction.

The visionaries or Seers referred to here were just a paradigmatic few of those who continued a ministry of prophetic guidance and counsel to the kings and the people until the time of the exile into Babylon.[1] II Chronicles 29 tells us that it was such Seers that supervised the religious education that the Levites provided the people throughout the nation of Israel. It was Seers who wrote the liturgies for worship in Solomon's temple. A Seer named Asaph wrote many of the celebrative Psalms that were intended for and used in the formal national worship services. One has the impressions that these prophetic Seers were the professors of theology and religion and the leading creative artists of the day. All their fellow citizens seemed to know intuitively that the Seers' wisdom and

---

1. See II Chronicles 16:10, 33:18-19, 35:15, Isaiah 29:10, Isaiah 30:10, Amos 7:12, Micah 3:7,

creativity was a result of the fact that "the spirit of the Lord had come upon them." They were visionaries because they were those who lived life open to the Holy Spirit and "close to the wind" of the divine breath in the world. They were no different or magically special from those who similarly seek God in our day.

Joel was a prophet and visionary who lived after the Babylonian exile, probably around 400 BCE. Joel's most dramatic and memorable vision is expressed in Joel 2:28, in which he declares that the visionary capabilities of the Seers is a thing to be sought and emulated in every age by those who highly prize authentic spirituality. It is not something to be seen as magical and restricted to ancient times or biblical inspiration. Human paranormal experiences in any age, says Joel, are strong intimations that God is relating to us in the spirit. When we have such experiences we can count on the prophetic promise.

> You shall know that I am in the midst of my people;
> That I, the Lord, am your God, and there is no other.
> And it shall come to pass . . . that I will pour out my spirit upon all flesh.
> Your sons and daughters shall receive paranormal intimations of the spirit,
> Your old men shall dream dreams; your young men shall see visions.
> Even upon your hired men and women will I pour out my spirit.
> (JHE trans)

There certainly seem to be no exceptions to the human community which has access to the divine spirit. It is, apparently, simply a matter of sailing close to the wind, keeping our spirits open to the spirit of God. Clearly the invitation seems to be as universal as God's promised grace. That would confirm the word of the prophet Jeremiah who has God promising, "If with all your heart you truly seek me, you shall ever surely find me" (Isa. 29:13).[2]

Do you suppose that applies to visionaries of today? Almost certainly we should assume that we can count on the divine spirit today as at any other time. William James reported in his Gifford Lecture that

---

2. Translation by Felix Mendelssohn, *Elijah, An Oratorio*, Section Number 4, Tenor Aria, New York: G. Schirmer, Inc. In J. Harold Ellens, *Understanding Religious Experience, What the Bible Says About Spirituality*, Westport, CT: Praeger, 2008), p. 105, this reference was erroneously given as a translation in G. F. Handel's *Messiah*.

many of the persons he interviewed regarding their experiences with the divine spirit spoke of several times when they felt the consciousness of a presence that felt as intense as standing in a fulmination of inner warmth.[3] John Wesley reported that when he finally came to sense within him the deep reassurances of God's grace to him, it felt like an uncommon level of intensity and inner warmth.

The person whom James cited, later said that he had not merely had a consciousness of something present, but sensed that there was "fused in the central happiness of it, a startling awareness of some ineffable good." This was not the vague emotional effect that one gets from reading a poignant poem or viewing a strikingly beautiful scene, nor was it like the sense of transport one may achieve while listening to magnificent music. It was instead a "sure sense of knowledge of the close presence of a sort of mighty person, and after it went, the memory persisted as the one perception of reality. Everything else might be a dream, but not that" (James, 63).

James has a very long quotation from a clergyman who reported that he remembered an evening when he was taking a leisurely walk on a hill when his "soul opened out" to God and there the world of the infinite and of the mundane rushed together. The depth of his own struggle with life opened to the unfathomable depth of the transcendent world. He stood under the stars and "all the beauty of the world, and love, and sorrow, and even temptation, flooded him with a sense of the presence of the creator God." He had not sought for this but felt a perfect union of his own spirit with the spirit of God. He lost all sense of the ordinary things around him. "For the moment nothing but an ineffable joy and exaltation remained." He felt it was impossible to describe the experience but the effect was like that of some great orchestra "when all the separate notes have melted into one swelling harmony that leaves the listener conscious of nothing save that his soul is being wafted upwards, and almost bursting with its own emotion" (67).The narrator continued. There in the quiet darkness he felt a presence he could not see, but he could no more "have doubted that *He* was there than that I was. Indeed, I felt myself to be, if possible, the less real of the two. My highest faith in God and truest idea of him were then born in me. I have stood upon the Mount of Vision since, and felt the Eternal round about me. But never since has there come quite the same stirring of the heart. Then, if ever, I

---

3. William James, *The Varieties of Religious Experience*, (New York: Morrow, 1958).

believe, I stood face to face with God, and was born anew by his spirit" (James, 67–68). James fills twenty five pages of his book reporting such narrations regarding the reality of the unknown.

My own illumination at age seven when I was filled with an enormous sense of relief and meaning, feeling entirely filled with the new sense of purpose and calling to ministry, is very nearly the same kind of experience as the clergyman explained to James.

It was accompanied, for me, with a life encompassing sense of wellbeing, light that connected heaven and earth, a joyful fullness of the meaning of everything, and utter clarity. It rendered my life permanently tranquil regarding the impasse of mental and spiritual darkness in which I had been enshrouded for two solid years. Such moments have become more, rather than less, frequent as my life unfolds. Each one of those events has had to do with a remarkable intervention in my life involving an experience and illumination that either changed my life dramatically or drew me into a course of action that radically changed the life of someone else who badly needed just that, just then.

In 1976 Julian Jaynes, a professor of psychology at Princeton University, published a wonderfully intriguing and evocative book with a long and complicated title, *The Origin of Consciousness in the Breakdown of the Bicameral Mind*.[4] Obviously, by the term bicameral mind, he means to refer to the fact that our brains are divided into two hemispheres. We have a right brain and a left brain. The left brain is that hemisphere that processes experience mainly in terms of linear logic, problems solving, finely crafted sentences, and bottom line thinking. It is through these kinds of experiences that people with predominant left brain function get most of their meaning out of life. They tend to be people who like logical arguments, relatively rigid predictability, fixed faucets, solved problems, law and order, and a well regulated life. They tend to be rigid, habitual, controlled, and controlling.

The right brain serves another purpose and works quite differently. It is the hemisphere that generates language resources; and processes experience in terms of sensations of color, texture, form, shape, a sense of mass, aesthetic qualities, emotions, and relationships. People who are right-brain-dominant process the meaning of life in terms of such values, expectations, and perceptions.

---

4. Julian Jaynes, *The Origin of Consciousness in the Breakdown of the Bicameral Mind* (Boston: Houghton Mifflin, 1976).

Seventy percent of the males in the world are left-brain-dominant, and seventy percent of the females in the world are right-brain-dominant. The remaining thirty percent of both genders tend to be high on both scales, a capacity that tends to lead to better and healthier adjustment in life and to less turbulent relationships. This pattern is confirmed by many studies of brain preference, but notably in numerous superb works by Restak, Edwards, Springer and Deutsch.[5]

Jaynes' take on all this information has to do with life in the spirit. He argues persuasively that human beings have always had surprisingly greater paranormal ways of knowing than people today realize. Since the resurrection and restoration of Aristotle's scientific method to the human quest for knowledge of the material world, humans have been preoccupied with empirical science. The empirical or scientific method proved to be very productive. It created the world as we know it.

The resulting difficulties, however, were at least two. While formerly people were approximately equally interested in rational idealism and its speculation about the spiritual world, after Bacon the Western World shifted its interest to tangible mechanics and its products. This shift of focus to issues of cause and effect, and away from matters of meaning and purpose amounted to a very major psychospiritual change. It included a loss of interest in paranormal ways of knowing, in favor of a virtually exclusive interest in empirical ways of knowing: logic, factor analysis, and rational empiricism. The shift left the human spirit hungry for contact with meaning and purpose issues, the domain of the spirit.

Jaynes raised major concerns about this already decades ago, and it has subsequently become the main problem that is addressed by the Post-Modern movement in philosophy, psychology, sociology, and religious studies. Jaynes' argument centers in his claim that the dominant character of the human meaning-quest for most of history was carried out on the spiritual plain. His voluminous evidence warrants his conclusion that humans did not depend primarily upon the analytic or logical abilities until a millennium or two before the days of Julius Caesar, Jesus,

---

5. Richard M. Restak, *The Brain, The last Frontier* (New York: Warner, 1979); Restak, *The Brain Has a Mind of Its Own, Insights From a Practicing Neurologist* (New York: Harmony, 1991); Restak, *The Brain* (New York: Bantam, 1984); Restak, *Receptors* (New York: Bantam, 1994); Restak, *The Modular Brain* (New York: Scribners, 1994); Betty Edwards, *Drawing on the Right Side of the Brain* (Los Angeles: Jeremy P. Tarcher 1989); Sally P. Springer and Georg Deutsch, *Left Brain, Right Brain* (New York: Freeman, 1981 and 1985).

and Josephus. They did not trust their left brains primarily, as we do today. They trusted their right brains and as a result, lived life continually listening to and obeying the voices of the gods that they perceived they heard in their affective brain hemisphere.

This meant that people were primarily interested in the meaning and purpose issues in understanding life, and so they were tuned to the paranormal ways of knowing more than to the empirical ways of knowing, associated with the left brain function. That is, intuition, ESP, and prescience had more value to them and were trusted more by them as sources of the knowledge that was valuable and useful. Jaynes is sure that it was that orientation that made it possible for the ancient Hebrew prophets, visionaries, and Seers to hear the word of the Lord and convey it to the society. They possessed highly functional right brains, which generated the insights of transcendental meaning evident to them in many situations in life. They functioned with high degrees of ESP, intuition, and prescience, and they trusted them.

They lived life close to the wind. They were consciously and intentionally open to the visitations of the divine spirit. They expected to experience revelations, intuitions, and extrasensory perceptions of the presence, nature, and meaning of God; and so when those experiences came to them, they recognized them readily for what they were. They had no scientific resistance to them, but rather considered them more natural and real than conclusions drawn from empirical assessment or analytical problem solving. They heard the word of the Lord in their right brains.

Jaynes insists that these same capacities are still as real in humans today, despite the scientific revolution, but we have repressed them in favor of empirical science. We have allowed them to atrophy and so we are not awake to our paranormal and psychospiritual potentials, as people used to be and we should be. We are afraid of them, denigrate them, downplay them, and do not trust them. Thus we do not have an expectation of the spirit's communication with us, we do not create a consciousness of the spirit's presence, and so we do not cultivate a divine spirit-oriented culture. We are afraid to share with others the moments when we have experiences that can be accounted for in no other way than as a divine illumination. If we do share them, we expect others to think we are psychologically whacky.

Thus we never get to the point of naming such moments as "of the spirit." Consequently, we do not collect the series of memories of such events that have happened to us in our lives. So we lose our collective cumulative awareness of the intensity with which the divine spirit is always present to us. We lose out on forming life into a culture of spirit-consciousness. It is imperative that we begin again to value this side of human life, experience, and the meaning quest. We have lost so much of our awareness and experience of the presence of God. We really should try again to live life close to the wind—to the (*ruach*) breath of the spirit.

Edgar Cayce was known to those around him as a gifted professional photographer, a friendly Presbyterian Sunday School teacher, and the "sleeping prophet." Hugh Lynn Cayce wrote the introduction to *The Complete Books of Edgar Cayce, Modern Prophet*,[6] a volume containing the "sleeping prophet's," four published works. He makes the following observations.

His own family knew him as a wonderful husband and father. The "sleeping" Edgar Cayce was an entirely different figure; a psychic known to thousands of people, in all walks of life, who had cause to be grateful for his help; indeed, many of them believe that he alone had either saved or changed their lives when all seemed lost. The "sleeping" Edgar Cayce was a medical diagnostician, a prophet, and a devoted protagonist of Bible lore (7).

The author of a PhD dissertation about Cayce's life and work referred to him as a religious Seer. He was born in 1877 and already in childhood seemed to possess powers of perception which exceeded the normal range of the senses. He reported, as a child, the ability to see and converse with what he called visions, frequently of dead relatives. While still very young he was able to develop a photographic memory of textbook material if he first entered a kind of sleep trance. In his twenties he experienced an affliction of his throat muscles that made speaking difficult. He asked a friend to induce a hypnotic sleep or trance, and in that state he was able to diagnose his own problem, prescribe medication and physical therapy, and so cure himself. He lived consciously and intentionally close to the wind of the divine spirit.

---

6. Hugh Lynn Cayce, ed., *Edgar Cayce, Modern Prophet* (New York: Gramercy, 1990).

This event led to physicians seeking him out for diagnostic consultation. If given the name and address of a patient he could telepathically diagnose the condition and prescribe treatment at a distance, wherever he was. This was documented by Wesley Ketchum, MD, in a clinical report to the learned societies in medicine; and a popularized description of these unorthodox medical processes appeared in *The New York Times* for 09 October 1910. Thereafter, he was sought out by suffering humans from all over the country. After his death on 03 January 1945, it was discovered that he had left a record of over 8000 telepathic-clairvoyant diagnoses over a forty year period. He called them "readings." They were always produced by him while in a kind of sleep trance.

His capacity to discern human suffering from afar, telepathically diagnose and heal it, focus the eye of the soul, so to speak, upon seeking the will and spirit of God, seems remarkably like the biblical prophets. Quite apart from his mystical functions as a Seer, Cayce was known as a man who lived his life open to the divine spirit from childhood to death at seventy-eight years of age. Sailing close to the wind, in that sense, he seems to have been in touch with the spirit of God, as were Isaiah, Hosea, Jeremiah, Micah, Amos, and Joel. He regularly had paranormal experiences of illumination and epiphany like those to which the biblical prophetic figures testify. The benefit he afforded other people's lives in his trance-states of insight, as well as the quality of his own personal character itself, strongly urges the conclusion that his sense of the presence of the divine spirit in his experience was of the same nature as that experienced by Jesus.

Edgar Cayce's experience fits neatly into the hypothesis of Julian Jaynes, namely, that the right brain, and thence the unconscious mind, are channels for the intimations of the divine spirit. Hypnosis and dreams are the two ways that we have of accessing the content of our unconscious minds. Dreams are always the processes of the unconscious mind sorting out the chaos of material dumped into that huge seething vat, as life experiences come at us faster or with greater trauma than we can handle at the time, with our conscious minds. All dreams are, therefore, of great importance. All dreams mean something important about our inner psychic state. All dreams are attempts by our unconscious to get time on the conscious mind's "computer," so to speak, to sort out the material the unconscious mind needs to process in order to keep us sane and well ordered in our inner selves.

This is the way our unconscious reduces our anxiety, distractions, emotional confusion, and inner anguish. Running this material on the conscious mind's computer makes it possible for our unconscious to select out the important stuff to store in our memory, discard the unimportant stuff, and call critical matters to our attention. Dreams take place, normally, while we are asleep because that is when the mind's computer is available. Usually when it comes to the critical matters to be drawn to our attention, our unconscious awakens us from sleep so we can remember that material from the dream.

It is completely understandable, in Jaynes' model, that Cayce and prophets from time immemorial, such as Samuel, Daniel (7:13), Ezekiel, Peter, and other biblical figures, experienced the revelations from God through their unconscious, processed in their right brains, in the form of dreams. That is where the action is. That is the channel through which the spirit speaks.

We are forced to conclude, by reason of the numerous figures like Moses, Samuel, Isaiah, Hosea, Jesus, Paul, Aurelius Augustine, Thomas Aquinas, Julian of Norwich, Deepak Chopra, Edgar Cayce, and the like, with which history is studded, that Julian Jaynes is correct in his claim that the availability of the intimations of the divine spirit is no less intense, no less likely, and no less revealing in our day than it was in the biblical era. If we see it less and sense it less it has something to do with the decreased keenness with which we are tuned to the right brain and hence to the spirit of God, in this day of empirical science.

The wisdom and operational value of such Gurus as Sathya Sai Baba of Putaparthi, India, on the one hand, and many persons of courage and wisdom whom we often take for granted in our present moment in the Western World, on the other, tend to generate confidence and a sense of credibility in their followers because they offer both guidance and counsel that is immediately applicable to daily life. Sai Baba's wisdom is universalistic, in that it embraces all humanity, indeed, all the world of living things. He counsels an ethic of passion and compassion. He seems to have distilled the best, the most godly, and the most humane aspects of Hinduism, Buddhism, Christianity, Islam, and Judaism and integrated them into one wholistic theological worldview. Can we really avoid saying that such a force for good in the world in our day is not "of the spirit" of God?

In this regard, Sai Baba's message is much like the inclusive emphasis of Ba'hai. It is easy to sense that such a figure really does have something from the divine spirit. One can readily sense that he has lived his 80 years with his soul open to God, and with his intentional and conscious life-focus set close to the wind of the spirit, so to speak. He, himself, claims to be a kind of incarnation of the divine spirit, as was Jesus, and certain other Avatars whom he identifies as having lived this same revelatory life before Jesus and between the time of Jesus and himself. Avatars are, in eastern religious perspective, something like completed spirits, fully in touch with and incarnating the divine spirit to as great an extent as a human person can.[7]

Deepak Chopra is much better known in the Western World than is Sai Baba, and is very popular among a large following of disciples or readers today because he has said essentially the same thing as Julian Jaynes. However, he has made his claim on the basis of his own personal experience and spiritual worldview, rather than on the basis of Jaynes' kind of psycho-historical science. His popularity arises out of the fact that when he speaks of the dynamics of spirituality and the divine spirit that humans need so much and miss so easily, his invitation to live life close to the wind of the spirit rings true to the deepest hungers in human hearts, minds, and souls.

Ken Wilber's assessment of Chopra's work and wisdom is highly positive. Wilber is the dean of all psychologists with an understanding of and extensive research in the human capacity for paranormal ways of knowing.[8] He declares that "Deepak Chopra has introduced literally millions of people to the spiritual path, and for this we should all be profoundly grateful. In *How to Know God*,[9] Deepak continues his pioneering outreach, showing that God consciousness unfolds in a series of stages, each important and remarkable in itself, yet each getting closer to Source" (fly leaf).

---

7. Charlene Leslie-Chaden, *A Compendium of the Teachings of Sathya Sai Baba* (Prasanthi Nilayam: Sai Towers Publishing, 1996).

8. Ken Wilber, *The Spectrum of Consciousness* (Wheaton, IL, Madras, London: The Theosophical Publishing House, 1977); Wilber, *The Atman Project, A Transpersonal View of Human Development* (Wheaton, IL, Madras, London: The Theosophical Publishing House, 1980); Wilber, *No Boundaries, Eastern and Western Approaches to Personal Growth* (Boulder and London: Shambala Press, 1981).

9. Deepak Chopra, *How to Know God, The Soul's Journey Into the Mystery of Mysteries* (New York: Harmony, 2000).

Chopra thinks reality exists as a sandwich, in three layers. The layer of material reality we know fairly well and our five senses give us that knowledge. The middle layer is the quantum domain, in his words, which names a transition zone where energy turns into matter and vice versa. The third layer is the virtual domain, the place beyond time, space, and materiality; and it is the source of the origin of the material world. The human brain, according to Chopra, is designed to apprehend the layer of material reality, but also has a longing and proclivity to explore the other two layers. Because of our limited capacity to do so, we can never know exactly, intellectually or empirically, what we mean when we use the term, God. However, we do have the capacity to experience the presence of God's spirit, without being able to define or describe it tangibly; and we do not need to define or describe the experience of the divine spirit in our spirits in order for it to be real.

Chopra offers numerous vivid examples of serendipitous experiences humans have which provide clear messages of guidance or affirmation for us in life. Chopra prefers to think of visionaries as saints rather than just Seers or prophets. He makes the important point that such saints, those who live life close to the wind of the spirit, who hold life open to the pressures and presence of God's spirit, are not just *saintly*. We really *are saints*! Saints are folks who live a life full of God, full of love, full of compassion, full of forgiveness, not because they know this is the right thing to do but because they cannot help themselves. They automatically are overflowing with forgiveness, love, and compassion. That is what incarnation of the divine spirit entails. Living close to the wind becomes one's inner nature.

The true visionary's perception of divine illumination, says Chopra, is the acknowledgement that "The world has a heart, and that heart is love. In the midst of all struggle, I see that God is watching. He doesn't interfere, but he doesn't lose track, either. He brings a solution to fit every problem, a reaction that suits every action. How he does this is a mystery, but nothing is more real. There is grace in the fall of a leaf. Our deeds are weighed in the balance by a loving Creator, who never judges or punishes."[10] The unique experience of the visionary is not belief in, but clarity about these things. Chopra illustrates this with a story of a young man's enlightenment, which I borrow here because it is so exactly the same story of illumination we read repeatedly from every century,

10. Chopra, Op. Cit., 197.

culture, and religious tradition. James' work is full of stories so similar to this that one must conclude that this experience is a paradigm of an important and universal form of the experience of the manifestations of the divine spirit to a hungry human soul.

> A young man in his twenties named Bede Griffiths had been going through a period of deep doubt and depression. Being religious, he sought solace in a church, where he prayed without success. One day during service he heard the line. "Open my eyes that I may see the wondrous things out of Thy law": from the 113th Psalm. Deeply moved, the young man felt his melancholy lift away, and he had the overwhelming sense that his prayers had been answered by divine intervention. He walked outside onto the London streets, and later described the experience in the following words:

"When I went outside, I found that the world about me no longer oppressed me as it had done. The hard casing of exterior reality seemed to have been broken through, and everything disclosed its inner being. The buses in the streets seemed to have lost their solidity and were glowing with light. I hardly felt the ground as I trod . . . I was like a bird that had broken the shell of its egg and finds itself in a new world; like a child that has forced its way out of the womb and sees the light of day for the first time" (204).

I could recite numerous similar narratives from the files of my clinical practice, as I am sure any therapist can, who is sensitive to the psychospiritual dimensions of the human quest. I remember especially the story of a friend of mine, an intensely spiritual and sensitively articulate woman in her middle years, who had spent some earlier time in treatment for depression. After a considerable time of analysis it seemed clear that her condition was not so much systemic and biochemical as it was situational. This led her to review her relationship with her ex-husband from whom she had experienced a traumatic divorce, her unusually difficult relationship with her father in adolescence, and her sense of devaluation, demeanment, and loneliness.

She reported that she had lived in this oppressive psychospiritual state for many years, feeding off the rage she felt to the primary male figures in her life, and consequently unable to form any constructive new relationships to relieve her sense of being utterly alone. On the one hand, she wished to resolve the impasse with her father that had developed mainly from her having been a seriously unconventional, oppositional, self-defeating, and rebellious adolescent. She had wasted her life, her sexuality, her education, her time, her health, and her relationships. She felt that she had dug a ditch too deep for her to transcend. She had long since abandoned the religious traditions of her family, and the spiritual quest it had offered her.

Then one day, in desperation, feeling overtly suicidal, she walked into Christ Church Cranbrook, in the middle of the day, in the middle of the week. The cathedral was empty and cool. She sat in a pew near the back with her head on her arm on the pew ahead of her. She wept pitiably. When she opened her eyes they fell upon the Book of Common Prayer. She picked it up and it fell open to the passage, "Knowest thou not that of thine own self thou canst do nothing?" She began immediately to feel an intense sense of release and relief at the center of her being. This was accompanied by a physical warmth that started in the center of her chest and grew from a walnut to an orange, from an orange to a cantaloupe, from a cantaloupe to a watermelon and then it pervaded her entire self: material and spiritual.

Just then she remembered words of her father expressing forgiveness and compassion to her somewhere back there in her rebellious years when she was trying to define herself by defying him. Over the next days, she said, she felt like everything in her being had changed. Her depression disappeared immediately and completely. Her sense of enthusiasm for her life sprang up resiliently. Her appetite returned. Her health seemed renewed. She longed for each new opportunity to return to church. She felt in every way like she had finally come home—to her self—and to the divine spirit. Even her sorrow over her wasted life percolated out of her and she felt an immense sense of gratitude for the road along which she had so lately come and for the illumination into which just that rough road had finally led her, out of the wilderness and into the clearing.

This is not so remote from my own experiences of illumination. From those moments my body felt light, my spirit clarified, my life hopeful and on a good track. It was not so much as though something was cured; but rather that everything had changed. Everything about me had changed. A new spirit had been injected into me. The divine spirit is alive and well in our day and awaiting the moment to encounter us with spiritual intimations.

Such moments of clarity may come and go, rise and fall, intensify and dissipate. Keeping ourselves consciously intentional about opening life and heart to the divine spirit, however, can empower us to maintain a consistent level of spiritual awareness and openness to the intimations from God. Sometimes our paranormal experiences of the spirit seem to transcend time and materiality and when we become aware again of the things around us, we wonder where the time has gone. Frequently, we feel disoriented for a few moments until we catch our breath, so to speak.

Such suspension from time and materiality may happen in the intense experience of making love, in captivation by a grand piece of music, in a particularly illumining worship service, or in sitting in an art gallery contemplating a truly great painting, or in direct paranormal intimations from God. All these are moments of the spirit's presence.

No one was ever wrestled into the kingdom of God by logical argument, but no one ever needs to be. Any human being, given the chance to see the genuineness of his or her own spiritual hunger, and the authenticity of the intimations of the divine spirit, those with the eyes to see and ears to hear, will come away discerning with great relief that this is the source of wholeness for the human spirit.[11]

---

11. Parts of this chapter appeared in a substantially different form in J. Harold Ellens, *Understanding Religious Experiences, What the Bible Says About Spirituality* (Westport, CT: Praeger, 2008).

6

Appointments with God

Every human's life is marked by numerous events of which it is difficult to discern whether they are accidental, serendipitous, or providential. The older I get the more I find myself inclined to see such moments as appointments with God. That is not because I am now inclined, in my later years, to think in terms of death and transcendence. It has nothing to do with that at all. Though I am nearly 80, I expect to live another 20 years or so. That is an entire career! Do we not all think ourselves invincible? Everyone else can die, but surely not me, not now, not for a long time!

No, I am inclined to see such inadvertencies as appointments with God because I cannot account for their content in any other way. Those moments seem always to have had a divine or transcendent dimension as they unfolded in my life. It is easy for me to illustrate this fact persuasively, I think. Let me ease into it and present progressively more compelling narratives of how this has unfolded in my life.

Some paranormal experiences of the spirit are not attended by extraordinary or dramatically surprising events and are more internal processes of individual subjectivity than external processes of overt objectivity. Many such occasions had life-shaping effects upon me over the years.

My father lived with the conscious experience of paranormal processes and events every day. He was a man of deep personal faith who discerned the presence of the divine spirit in life as a regular and normal aspect of every day. On our 60 acre family farm he kept a modest herd of dairy cattle, a hundred chickens, and a couple families of domestic pigs. These were fed from the hay, corn, and oats we raised on the farm. In turn, these animals supplied our family of eleven with the essentials of nutritious living during the days of the Great Depression and WW II.

In addition, the supply of eggs and cream provided enough cash to pay for the groceries we could not grow in our large garden, orchard, and berry patches. When we had occasion to sell a veal calf or a few pigs, we had cash for medical bills, clothing, auto and farm machinery repairs, seeds for planting, and fertilizers and insecticides. We never managed to get enough to paint the barn. I remember what a momentous thing it was when my mother was able to get a fine watch and repair her wedding ring from which an opal had fallen.

It was in any case, and most of the time, a precarious balance between just enough and acknowledged want. A bad year was not just an idea for us. It was a palpably experienced operational reality, a chronic feeling in the pit of our stomachs. Therefore, it is understandable that when the rains did not come on time, my father's solution was to pray for rain. I remember walking out into our 10 acre corn field with my father one day in July 1937 when drought threatened the crop and he said, "Listen, you can hear the corn burning up on the stalk." He prayed. It rained. We were saved for that year.

We had a neighbor who had a much larger farm than we and considerably less interest in the things of the spirit, so far as we could tell. He was a jovial and enjoyable sort of guy. He liked humor and practical jokes and apparently lived what my parents seemed to me to think of as a slightly reckless sort of life. However, he did as well as the rest of us, and he always teased my father about praying for rain. He claimed he was an atheist and he seemed at least to be quite secular. He seemed quite sure one could squeeze enough meaning from life without taking God into account. He suggested that weather was the most obvious evidence that the world operated arbitrarily in terms of its own meteorological dynamics, that weather patterns were determined by forces in the air that we could not discern or predict, and that divine intervention had nothing to do with it.

My father prayed for rain and, of course, eventually it rained. Our neighbor argued that it would have rained eventually in any case. It always does eventually. Even in the Kalahari desert eventually it rains—a quarter of an inch every ten years or so. In McBain, Michigan it rains rather more often than that, but not because some African Bushman did the rain dance or my father prayed for rain. It was all a matter of nature's whims—or rather of the natural laws of weather, our neighbor contended.

Well, that was an interesting, congenial dialogue my father carried on with our neighbor, sometimes with turns of great humor thrown in. It became clear to us as children, as well as to our neighbor's children, that my father believed in a rather rich and enriching form of divine providence prevailing in all of life, and our neighbor believed in a kind of tragi-comical fate that shaped our destiny. So there was one fundamental difference between our family and our neighbor's—and it made all the difference in the world.

Drought did not drive us to doubt but to an intense awareness of our direct dependence upon the presence and benevolence of God in our lives. It was clear to us from whence the blessings of life came to us, and so we prayed. When the rain came and the crops flourished and the flocks and herds were refreshed, we received that rain as a blessing. Moreover, we knew that it had come to us from our provident God. It made us all glad and profoundly grateful. We read the Bible where it says that God sends his rain on the just and the unjust. We were not always sure where we stood in that equation, but we knew from where the rain came. It became a metaphor of just about everything else in our lives, of course. Life was, for us, largely a state of gratitude.

Our neighbor took quite a different view of it all. It did not seem to trouble him much, but I never noticed that tone of persistent gratitude as a way of life, in his experience or expression. It seemed more like life was just a thing to be lived through as best one could, keeping a stiff upper lip, so to speak, and finding as much humor in it all as possible. I often felt sad about the difference it made for his children, who seemed not to deal in the deep meaning of life that kept me going most of the time. That is what I mean in saying that the difference turned out to make all the difference in the world.

Now it is easy to say that my father's perspective was merely the mythology of his faith that conveyed itself rather naturally to the rest of us in the family and formed our way of looking at things. The only thing wrong with that statement is one word—merely. It was not *merely* his "I believe" concept, which is the definition of the word—myth. It was also a real mediation of the divine spirit that is pervasive throughout the universe, and it tuned up our lives to genuine sensitivity to our own spirits as the presence of that divine spirit to us. In that sense, the shaping influence of my father's perspective, in which my mother also participated intensely, was the action of the spirit of God conditioning our lives to a persistent spirit of optimistic gratitude, and confident security. That is the way in which it is a paranormal experience, that is, an experience of life as not merely secular process but as a matrix in which the divine spirit persistently acts with us, even through our rather fanciful mythologies. They open a channel for the spirit to employ.

So you see, that is why I mentioned earlier that some paranormal experiences of the spirit are not attended by extraordinary or dramatically surprising events; and are more internal processes of individual subjectivity than external processes of overt objectivity. Nonetheless, they become channels through which the sacred spirit of God acts in and upon our lives. Now you see what I mean when I say that many such occasions had life-shaping effects upon me over the years.

The year 1945 was an especially grievous year for me. I was 12 when, in the month of February my eldest brother was drafted into the war. My father went around to a number of government authorities to find out if it were possible for my brother to sign up with the Coast Guard or the Merchant Marine instead of going into the infantry, assuming that doing so would place him in a less lethal combat service-support unit than directly in a combat unit. I do not know if it was my father's ultimate conclusion or my brother's, but he accepted the draft call and entered infantry squad and platoon training at Camp Joseph T. Robinson, near Little Rock, Arkansas in April.

He wrote letters home regularly. We awaited them in tears, read them in tears, and hoped he would never need to actually do the things he described he was being trained to do. His particular company was trained to deploy into a specific section of the town of Osaka, Japan. They trained in temporary buildings and streets, like movie sets, designed to look exactly like the scenes they would encounter in Osaka. It was expected that they would encounter desperate hand to hand combat, taking the city building by building, street by street; the worst kind of combat demanded of soldiers.

Good military leaders see cities as obstacles to gaining military objectives, not good objectives in themselves; and they outflank them as much as possible. However, General MacArthur had announced that the Japanese military and civilians would defend their homeland desperately and to the death, and that we would lose a million of our men and kill seven million Japanese before we could subdue Japan, if we had to invade it to bring the war to an end. Those who think ill of Truman for dropping the atomic bombs on Hiroshima and Nagasaki in the summer of 1945, have forgotten this fact. We killed 180,000 Japanese with those two bombs, instead of seven million; and we lost only a few of our own in the process. Those percentages are extremely recommendable. The naysayers should stop acting and talking like lunatics.

In any case, every day I prayed for my brother's survival. I prayed desperately. I was sure he would be one of those one million casualties. However, by an executive order, President Harry S. Truman made the wise and courageous decision, and dropped those bombs on Hiroshima on August 6 and on Nagasaki on August 9, 1945. My brother finished his training for the invasion of Japan on August 15, 1945. He came home to us for a 30 day leave before shipping to the Pacific. On September 2, while he was on leave, the war ended with the unconditional surrender and abject capitulation of Japan.

For six months I had prayed every day for his deliverance from the horrors of the potential invasion of Japan and from the very real threat of his death. My prayers intensified in fear and anguish as the days of August unfolded and his deployment loomed over us like an awful doom. I was still praying with great urgency on September 2, when we heard Gabriel Heater, the radio commentator, announce that the war had come to an end. I knew at that moment that this awesome event was a personal answer to my prayer.

Now if you are sensible, you will say that a lot of others were praying as well. Indeed, I am sure our entire nation was praying, and probably some worried mothers in Japan. Moreover, you should insist that there were a very lot of other dynamics that caused the war to end just then. All that is true! There was, nonetheless, a ministry of the divine spirit mediated to me personally through all those dynamics of anguish and imploration, during those six dread months. It was a subtle paranormal experience of God's spirit of which I savored the flavor in my own spirit. It is those kinds of things that make us what we are. Those are life-changing experiences that find the normal channels of life's unfolding to create the paranormal work of the divine spirit in our spirits. These kinds of experiences may not be seen as very extraordinary or dramatically surprising, but they change one's life. They are "moments of the Spirit."

One other illustration may suffice. I was the senior Protestant Chaplain at the Landstuhl Army Medical Center in the early 1960s.

When I was a year or so from completing my tenure at that post, I received an invitation from Princeton Theological Seminary to undertake an advanced degree in Second Temple Judaism and Christian Origins, known at that time as New Testament and Intertestamental Studies. The invitation said I would work with the world's premier New Testament textual scholar at that time, Professor Bruce M. Metzger.

I accepted the invitation and the small scholarship that came with it, not certain how I would support my family of five children for the two years of graduate study. My family and I committed the matter to prayer and to trust in the providence of God and the leading of God's spirit that had been the mode I had learned in my parents' home. We held confidently to the notion that we would experience those intimations and illuminations of the spirit that would be necessary for us to see our way ahead responsibly and comfortably.

We landed in New York and I was released from active duty at Ft. Hamilton. Relatives invited us to share their home while we got established. In six weeks I was approached by a church in New Jersey that had just lost its pastor, had had a previous successful experience with a pastor who had been an army chaplain, and urgently implored me to take up the ministry of their church. I did so, with gratitude, certain that this was an answer to our prayers. It turned out to be a gratifying and fruitful ministry, from which we established two daughter churches over the next four years and increased the size of the congregation by half at the same time. Those were idyllic years of spiritual and cultural growth for us.

Now one can account for the fortuitous coincidence of the church's need and my availability for it, as happy happenstance, of course. Moreover, to account for it that way would be accurate. One need not see such inadvertencies in life as miracles or supernatural events. However, that is beside the point. The point is that we prayed and the circumstances in our lives unfolded in such a way that our prayers were answered, just as in praying for rain or for my brother's safely. That point is a powerful point that should not be trivialized or rationalized away. For us, in our posture of faith, it was the way in which the divine spirit channeled God's providential presence to our lives and registered it in our spirits in such a fashion that it reinforced our sense of optimistic gratitude for the way in which God's world works.

C. S. Lewis is reported to have declared that at the moment we experience those subtle, life-changing experiences we know with certainty that they are "moments of the spirit," and then we spend the next six weeks rationalizing them away. Thus we trivialize our lives, shift these matters to superficiality, and fail to cultivate the culture of the Holy Spirit in our unfolding destinies. By naming those life-shaping events or processes as moments of the spirit, keeping track of them, sharing them with others who will also testify to such experiences and reinforce our own, we have in the end a master story of the ministry of the divine spirit in our spirits. It becomes a master story of the palpable ways that "we experience the illumining spirit", with a cumulative effect that cannot be otherwise better accounted for.

Other paranormal events in my life were, on the other hand, very dramatic providential interventions, unaccountable in any other way than the certainty that the divine spirit had intentionally arranged them. After I had retired from the US Army I was recalled to duty to help implement a mobilization plan that my team had developed during my assignment on the General Staff of the Health Services Command. I had two weeks to fine tune the plan, organize its manning and budgeting, and field the full program. We had tested the pilot a few years earlier.

I worked diligently to achieve my mission, using an outdated army computer with which I was not well acquainted. As the two weeks ran down to the final days, the plan was complete but needed to be edited and downloaded into the computer hard drive. I worked late into the night on the final Thursday of my allotted two weeks to complete the work. I had to be ready to open the retirement ceremony for a friend of mine the next morning. I was to check out that Friday noon to return home.

As I sweat my way through that evening and through putting the finishing touches to my program one of those sudden and intense thunder storms, so typical of the deep southwest, came boiling across Fort Sam Houston. It was just 2:00 AM when a fierce stroke of lightning blew through the office, extinguishing the electricity and burning out my computer. The entire two weeks of work in the computer was destroyed. I was bone tired and discouraged. I gave up, deciding to return home the next day to redo it all on my home computer and send it to the headquarters electronically. I locked the office, crossed the parade ground to my quarters, and fell into bed exhausted.

I was awakened in the early morning by the band playing on the parade ground to start the retirement ceremony. Groggy and stunned

I threw my self into the shower and then into my uniform and literally ran through the dim light of dawn to the parade field, only to find hundreds of soldiers doing PT at my end of the field. Circling around them I encountered a small group of female recruits huddled together and one of them was sobbing uncontrollably. I stopped to ask if I could help. Her companion said she had just gotten word from home that her girl friend had committed suicide, the 18th in that small Wisconsin town in three years. I had no time to sort things out for her so I pointed to the adjacent building and asked her to meet me there in my office at 10:00. I continued to the ceremony further down the field.

She came to the office at the appointed time and I was able to get her started on some useful intervention, and then I referred her to the Post Chaplain who cared for her successfully over the next six weeks. In the end she managed to handle her grief loss in a healthy manner. The chaplain reported to me later that this therapy process had been a significant turning point in the young lady's life.

If my computer had not crashed at 2:00 AM I would not have overslept. Had I awakened at the appropriate time, I would have walked to the retirement ceremony along the sidewalk as a dignified Colonel is expected to do. In that case I would have failed to encounter the needy young soldier and her needs would not have been met so efficiently as we were able to care for them. The healing change would not have occurred in her life, at least not as the divine spirit led out that process of intervention and growth, as we witnessed it.

It was clear to all of us at the time that this was a "moment of the Spirit." Through the inadvertent chain of events God acted healingly and shepherded that young woman to a life-changing experience in what could have been a psychospiritual tragedy for her. As I view that story in retrospect, it is clear to me that it was a completely unexpected and dramatically surprising paranormal event in which God acted overtly and palpably in the lives of all of us involved in that narrative, but particularly in the happenstances that were beyond our control. A brewing storm, a lightening strike, a fried computer, and a late alarm! If one has the eyes to see the reality that unfolded, the nature and meaning of it are clear and plain. The screen between the mundane and transcendent, between time and eternity, is permeable. The divine spirit acts overtly through it all the time. Perhaps it is appropriate to realize that the spirit is present to us all the time, and that that presence is only veiled from us by the fact that we exist here in one mode and the world of the divine spirit is present in a slightly different mode, just beyond our view. Then, in events like this one that presence is suddenly evident where we do not notice it ordinarily.

A similar, break-through, experience of the paranormal action of the divine spirit happened to me on an occasion when I was on my way to lecture in the Republic of South Africa. I flew from Detroit Metropolitan Airport to Kennedy Airport in New York. There I was to catch a South Africa Airliner to the Isle de Sol and on to Johannesburg, RSA. As I boarded that plane, the lady who was checking passports and tickets pulled me aside to inform me that my visa was not in order. I had spent a lot of time getting it sorted out correctly with the RSA Consulate in Chicago, so I was greatly surprised. I told her I was due to preach and lecture immediately upon arrival and could not delay my departure. She said that she could not board me. If she did the RSA government would fine the airlines $10,000, so I would need to go to the Consulate in NY and get the visa corrected. I gave her my card and took a taxi into the city.

When I reached the Consulate, my sense of urgency put the personnel there on the defensive and the harder I pushed the more they resisted. Finally, I was informed that they could not correct the visa and I would need to abort my trip. I phoned South Africa directly but nothing I attempted produced any gains. I left the Consulate forlorn. On the steps just outside the entrance I encountered an old friend who had been the former Vice-Consul in Chicago. It turned out he was now the Consul in New York and was returning from lunch. He was delighted to see me, as I him, and asked what was up. When I explained my predicament, he said it would be no trouble to straighten things out immediately. In ten minutes I had my new visa and a seat on the next flight, which happened to be so arranged that I would still arrive in the RSA in time for my schedule there.

With a light heart and a great sense of the surprising inadvertency in meeting my old friend who solved all problems quickly; I returned blithely to Kennedy Airport. When I entered the terminal the lady who had pulled me off the previous flight was standing by herself in a virtually empty loading area. I asked her where I could buy some flight insurance and she informed me that the insurance people had not shown up that day. Then she said, "Earlier you gave me your card. On it is says you are the director of the Christian Association for Psychological Studies.

What is this business of Christianity and Psychology?" I explained to her that my professional life had always been about the relationship between the two. She said, "I need to talk to you."

It turned out that the plane for which I was waiting to fly to Johannesburg was delayed two hours by weather. She was waiting to board the passengers. So she and I spent the two hours talking about the burden of her heart. She launched into it quickly, "I was born out of wedlock to a Dutch woman and an American soldier. I was rejected by both and raised in orphanages." Passed from one care-taker to another, she was eventually placed with foster parents. After being abused, neglected, and sexually molested in one home after another, she finally ran away at age 16, fled to a distant city, and found a way to raise herself. She enrolled in school, went on to college, and got a graduate degree.

She continued, "I have mastered four languages. I have the best job in the world, own a luxurious condominium in New York, collect lots of great art, and travel free anywhere I wish to go in the world. I have an ideal life now; but every morning when I wake up I want to kill myself." I asked her how old she was. She said she was 48. I spoke with her further about grief and loss, anxiety and depression, and envisioning some kind of realistic hope. None of this seemed to do much good, and I realized I was trying too hard to do too much in so short a time. I might never see her again. However, I noticed that her perception of my connecting with her fairly authentically, as the two hours made possible, and her sense of my caring for her enough to take the time, listen, and respond, made a difference to her. I told her I would write her from the plane and I would refer her to a friend of mine in New York City who was a psychiatrist, because I thought that she was experiencing the melancholia commonly associated with menopause and would profit from appropriate medication.

I followed up on my promise, wrote her from the plane, referred her to the psychiatrist whose office turned out to be near her home, and continued to write her occasionally for about six months. She did well with the treatment program, apparently, and wrote me a final letter about two years later to say she was well and happy and life was golden. I congratulated her and have not heard from her since that time. Obviously she is getting on well.

Tell me now, who messed up my visa? Was it accident, serendipity, benevolent providence, or the direct intervention of the divine Spirit? If my visa had not been a problem, I would not have handed her my card. Then she would not have reached out to me for help in her struggle with menopausal depression and suicidal ideations. If I had not encountered my friend on the steps of the Consulate, I would not have gotten my visa corrected. If he had not gotten me a seat on that second plane by putting a stand by student off that flight, I would not have seen her again. If the plane I was to catch had not been delayed two hours we would not have had time to talk. If it had been another plane to which I was assigned she would not have been the person there to board the passengers. It was a moment, indeed a long process, of the divine spirit's intervention.

By the presence and power of the all pervasive spirit in this world, God used the death of Esther to lead me into my life's calling. God used a lightening strike and a fried computer to lead me to a tragedy waiting to happen on the parade ground at Fort Sam Houston. God used a visa problem to place me in the right place and time to heal a badly abused soul. Are those experiences accident, serendipity, subtle providence, or overt divine intervention?

As I view my life in retrospect, it is clear to me that God does not cause little girls like Esther to die that awful death by fire, but God is not absent from that tragic event. God did not fry my computer but God was not absent from that discouraging moment and the events that followed so strangely upon it. God did not mess up my visa to South Africa but God was there.

As I look back I can see that the subtle but certain presence of the divine spirit brought me out of my stunned darkness in 1939 into the illumination of a purposeful destiny. That same spirit set me down in the dark dawn of a Texas morning next to a grieving little lady from a small Wisconsin town and gave her life new meaning. It was the divine spirit that used the bureaucratic inadvertencies of a visa problem to open the way to save the life of a woman who had suffered so much in trying to make sense of her abused life, only to have her biochemistry betray her at age 48. These paranormal moments of the divine redeeming spirit are much more normal that we think. We ought to keep track of them, name them for what they are, and cultivate a conscious culture of awareness of that perpetual pervasive presence.

7

A Voice in the Night, Truth Quests and Consolations

For the first 25 years of my professional life I was a minister in the Christian Reformed Church. In the early 1970s one of my elders accused me of the heresy of preaching and teaching that God loves every human being and intends all to be saved eternally. He put the matter into the judicial process of the denomination, which held to the notion, at least at the popular level, that before time began God had chosen a number of specific persons for heaven and consciously intended everyone else in the world and in history for eternal torture in hell.

The heresy trial went on for a couple of years before I was condemned on five counts, without being given an opportunity to speak for myself. The national Synod appointed a committee to meet with me for the purpose of removing my ordination, should I not recant. I felt enormous distress over an extended period of time while this matter unfolded. With the fatal committee meeting impending, I was exhausted but could not sleep. I had five children in college, one in a private high school, and my wife in graduate school. The loss of my ordination would result in the loss of my ministry, my salary, and my family's livelihood. It would be very difficult to find another opportunity for an appointment in ministry.

One night I found myself rolling around in bed sleeplessly, in fear and anxiety. Finally, at midnight I fell into the profoundly deep sleep of exhaustion. At 2:00 AM I was awakened by a loud voice in the room enjoining me to "Trust in the Lord and do good!" I sat bolt-upright in bed, blinked my bleary eyes as the thought went through my head that those words sounded like a biblical text. To graduate from the eighth grade I had had to memorize about 250 extended passages from the Bible, but I realized that this was not one of them. I took up my Bible and found the passage at Psalm 37:3. That psalm is not one a person is likely to memorize. It is a really bad psalm about slaughtering the wicked and destroying their children in the worst sort of way. But then right there in the third verse are these wonderful wise words.

The most remarkable thing about the voice in the night was the fact that the instant I heard that voice all my anguish was thoroughly removed from me. It was not that I heard the voice and decided to obey it and then felt better about everything. The anguish was lifted from my body and soul as though I had been cleansed by the voice. The suffering was completely taken away before I could even register the full import of the message. The agent of the voice had come to me unanticipated, uninvited, and had delivered me. From that minute forward I never had another moment of anxiety or fear about the matter of the trial or its potential destruction of my life, family, and ministry. All that pain and perplexity was simply removed from me.

Throughout the trial years I had continued to try to pastor my accuser as authentically as I could. He was a fairly psychopathological character and needed my care and friendship more than he realized. From the moment I heard the voice I went blithely on with my work, not thinking seriously again about the impending meeting with the committee from the Synod. I never tried to intervene to defend myself, since it was far too late in the game to do that in any case. However, the committee meeting was surprisingly delayed over the next ten months or year, by this and that inadvertency, and then my condemnation for heresy was set aside on a technical point, without my lifting a finger, so to speak.

From that moment my body felt light, my spirit clarified, my life hopeful and on a good track. It was not so much as though something was cured; but rather that everything had changed. Everything about me had changed. A new spirit had been injected into me. The divine spirit is alive and well in our day. The dramatic intervention of this theo*phony* was nearly as life-changing for me as the theo*phany* of my original illumination at age seven.

Four or five years later I moved from the Christian Reformed Church into the ministry of the Presbyterian Church (PCUSA) because of the failure of the former denomination to decide to ordain women. I have continued in ministry with the PCUSA for 30 years since then.

A subtler form of this kind of intimation of the divine spirit has more often occurred to me and to numerous others, bringing with it a pervasive infusion of hopefulness and consolation—a sense of having acquired a transcendental truth that changed life definitively. My father was a studious and serious minded boy with a deep sense of piety. He grew up in a very rural and relatively primitive setting, in the Christian Reformed Church in an immigrant community in Northern Michigan. In that intensely religious community the Canons of Dordrecht was a defining church document, with its doctrine of double predestination.

Double predestination is an ancient medieval dogma. It claims, as referenced above, that God decided from before history began that a large crowd of specific persons was chosen for eternal damnation in hell; while another assembly of individuals was chosen for eternal bliss in heaven. This was an arbitrary divine decision, and both the eternal state of the damned and of the elect for salvation supposedly served to enhance the glory of the omnipotent God, who can do and does as he pleases without any moral accountability.

Thus, as a genuinely pious prepubescent boy my father was already deeply troubled by the fear that he might be one of those whom God, in the eternal decrees he had established before he created the world, had chosen to consign to eternal damnation. My father described the effect upon him of this sense of arbitrary divine entrapment, as a dark cloud that hung over his head down to his eyes and made his whole world oppressive and sinister.

Life seemed to him during those early adolescent years like an inescapable spiritual doom that included an actual tangible experience of being physically and mentally repressed. Then one day, at age 14, he was sitting under the large oak tree in his parent's front yard, contemplating the sermon the preacher had preached the Sunday before. It focused upon the text from Romans 8 in which St. Paul declares that those whom God foreknew he also predestined to be conformed to the image of his son; . . . and those whom he predestined he also called, and those he called he justified, and those whom he justified he also sanctified. As that perception sank into his mind and heart, the darkness lifted from his head and heart quite suddenly, and he felt enormously free of all fear, guilt, and shame. He perceived that his own personal commitment to God and godliness counts in life, and God knows it in advance. "Those whom God foreknew . . . !" This affected God's eternal decree of predestination. From then on, my father testifies, he felt certain of his eternal salvation.

It would be possible to write off such an experience of life-changing spiritual illumination as merely the change that comes from a new cognitive insight—better information. However, I see no reason for such reductionism. When I consider the extent of life change that message in his mind and heart brought him, and the kind of godly man he was from that day until his death, I see every reason in the world for concluding that his illumination under that oak tree was a ministry of the divine spirit to him as surely as Buddha's under the Bodha Tree. Life is apparently filled with those kinds of moments for people whose lives are tuned to the spiritual frequency, who live their lives with the spiritual sail set close to the wind of the spirit. Surely the deliverance my father experienced was facilitated by the new insight he received from a Sunday sermon on Romans 8. But that became the channel by which he experienced more than a cognitive clarity. It became a channel for the divine spirit to effect a permanent spiritual life-change in my father's entire character and personality.

A friend of ours lost her policeman husband, quite suddenly, in the line of duty, when she was 34. She had a young child at the time. In her grief she found herself in a dilemma. She did not wish to remarry but she did not like to raise her son as an only child. She asked me to donate a sperm that she might have a second child. You can imagine that the contemplation of such a possibility at 65 years of age, was a critical consideration for me. I gave it a lot of thought for a long time. Her request cooked in my mind and heart for months. Then one morning I had the sense that I was being visited by an especially compelling force of urgency, indeed, necessity to make a decision. It was an imperative that came to me from somewhere outside of my person, as it were. It was an unequivocal directive to give her an answer. I felt as though the divine spirit was laying hold of me and insisting that the time had come for me to act on this. So I agreed to donate a sperm.

The sperm was appropriately applied and my friend immediately conceived. The child that she brought forth is a wonderful boy who is now 12 and growing into a magnificent, responsible young man. Any one around who understands the story agrees that this new life is a very special gift of the urgencies of the divine spirit. In my quandary, the spirit led me, clarified the course of action, and immediately made it fruitful. My sense of the spirit entering my spirit and urging me to act just at that moment in that manner and with such definitive effect, could not be a clearer demonstration of the fact that when we are open to the divine presence, the screen between the mundane and the transcendent is much more permeable than we usually think. Events of this sort are not adequately accounted for as happenstance or serendipity. These constructive, providential, life-changing moments are acts of God.

I left the active army chaplaincy after ten years of duty with the military, to accept a scholarship for further biblical studies under Professor Bruce M. Metzger at Princeton Theological Seminary. The confluence of our need and that of the church we came to pastor in Newton, New Jersey seem so obvious to us as a genuine providential leading of the spirit that we remember it vividly to this day. Such events shape lives and stand outside of the realm of events as humans can craft or manipulate them. These kinds of providential experiences are of the spirit, and if taken account of as such, form a fabric of divine guidance that permeates and becomes the inner structure of one's entire life.

This same sequence of events led to another quite remarkable shaping experience in my life. When I had finished most of the course work for my graduate degree under Metzger at Princeton, I was required to submit a proposal for my Masters Thesis. I did a great deal of research on the question of the authority of scripture as the ground for the Christian Faith and personal spirituality. When I thought I had explored that matter adequately, and my dear wife had typed 150 pages of carefully worked out research on the matter, I proposed to Metzger that I write on *The Authority of Scripture in Personal Faith Development*. Metzger looked at me for about a half minute, never looked at my prospectus at all, and said, "Well, I suppose you could write on that theme if you chose to do so, but you would need to move to either the Systematic Theology or Pastoral Theology Department to do that. We are not really interested in that question here in Biblical Studies." I was absolutely stunned. I could not believe I had heard him say that.

I thought deeply about his statement and it both troubled and intrigued me that he would hold such a position. I decided relatively soon that I would not write a thesis but would opt for the alternative provision of taking four extra courses instead of writing the Master's Thesis. This decision was based upon two considerations. First, I realized there must be a lot about New Testament (Biblical) Studies that I just did not yet get and so I should take as many more courses in the field as I could before completing my degree; and second, I did not really have the heart to present Metzger with another opportunity to turn me down so peremptorily and definitively. I use those adverbs to avoid the term, brutally.

After I had set myself on this new track instead of writing a thesis, I signed up for a course on the works of Philo and another on the biblical theology of Rudolf Bultmann, whose revolutionary New Testament Studies were just making a large impact in the United States. I also signed up for two courses in what we then called intertestamental studies and we now refer to as Second Temple Judaism. After a few weeks I gained the temerity to approach my other New Testament professor, Otto Piper, and put before him the question raised by Metzger's remarks. When he confirmed that in Biblical Studies there was no interest in the question of the authority of scripture, I asked him what was for him personally the ground and anchor of his Christian faith.

His response was winsome and quizzical. It has provoked in me a life time of quest for the grounding and orientation of true faith. Piper said, "Well, when you find that your own personal spiritual experience, and the witness of the church over the last 2000 years, and the message of the Bible all seem to ring true to one another, then I suppose you are on rather solid ground for the truth of the Christian faith." That set me on a trajectory of inquiry to understand my own inner self better and to understand better the biblical witness to the early developments of the Jesus movement. I had for decades by then been immersed in the theological traditions and testimonies of the historic church.

I left Princeton, upon completing my work under Metzger and undertook a PhD in the Psychology of Human Communication at Wayne State University, following it with a PhD in Second Temple Judaism and Christian Origins at the University of Michigan. Now the point that is important to me here is the fact that the concatenation of events around the completion of my ThM at Princeton, particularly those two sets of remarks by Metzger and Piper, resulted rather inadvertently in my taking four courses that set the course for the enormously gratifying journey of the rest of my life. Had my thesis not been rejected and had I not had that discussion with Piper, I would not have taken the courses on Philo, Bultmann, and Second Temple studies. Yet it was exactly those courses, and not the rest of my Princeton ThM that prepared me for the rest of my life's work. The rejection by Metzger set me on the pilgrimage to the research and writing of my most important book, *The Son of Man in the*

Gospel of John, and the enigmatic comment by Piper hastened me to my work in psychology.

This unanticipated and life-changing set of events unfolded, by the providential guidance and intimations of the divine spirit, in the way that led directly to the fulfillment of my destiny. It enriched my pastoral preaching and ministry, shaped the perspective of my university lecturing, and has been the quest that inspired all of my numerous publications. It is impossible to account for all the data in this sequence of events in a more rational way than to see this as divine intervention at each turn of the road. Moreover, the journey of my life continues to be filled with exactly these kinds of divine intimations and illuminations. It is exciting to share the numerous similar stories that form the warp and woof of my life. Some of those stories are as follows.

Our youngest daughter, who is now 44 years of age, is a doctor of veterinary medicine. In her last year of high school she suffered an extreme attack of mononucleosis. From that point on she was chronically troubled with various kinds of relatively exhausting disorders. At first the physicians called it Epstein Barr Syndrome. When that diagnosis no longer adequately managed the data of her troubles, they expanded the diagnosis to Fibromyalgia. She struggled on valiantly with sheer courage and force of will. Though she lost a year in medical school, she was able to make it up by her brilliance and ardor. Entering her medical practice, she suffered progressively more serious symptoms until at age 32 she was identified as having the ocular nerve lesion that is the definitive watershed criterion for the diagnosis of Multiple Sclerosis. She continues to suffer and to decline, now confined to a wheelchair, though she continues by sheer force of will to practice medicine and surgery. We are praying for a complete cure

These decades have been an ordeal for her, of course, and also for the rest of the family. The impact of it falls especially heavily on my wife who now cares for Brenda and her two children, 11 and 13, virtually full time day and night. This kind of support is crucial to assist Brenda in continuing her medical practice. Naturally, this is a weighty emotional and spiritual burden for me, as well, even though I am not as directly involved in Brenda's daily and hourly care as is Mary Jo. The impact that this has had on me took a curious and specific form. In my grief and pain at observing Brenda's grief and pain, and the way in which all that impacts my whole family, I felt increasingly distanced from my sense of the presence of God.

I have throughout my life had a relatively intense sense of the presence of God to me, at some moments more graphic than at others, but always gratifyingly empowering. Over the two or three years in which it became apparent that Brenda was failing rather rapidly and finally ended up permanently wheelchair-bound, it felt like God moved away. I do not believe it would be accurate to say that I was experiencing a decline in my faith or trust in God. I felt no loss of vigor in preaching the radical perspective on God's unconditional goodness and grace that has long been crucial to the meaning and consolation of my life, and the center of my world view.

I was not feeling a loss of faith but an increase of mystification in my heart and mind about how to handle, within that world view of trust and providence, the unaccountable suffering of my dear daughter. It made the God I knew from childhood up, seem now very far away. I lost the sense of the personal presence, and prayed fervently for its return. My parents had both died a decade or so before this, and now, with the departure of God from my immediate experience, I felt, with an unexpected weight, the experience of being orphaned. It seemed to me I was alone in life for the first time, with this unresolvable burden of my daughter's suffering, my helplessness to do anything to help her definitively, the shadow of her awful death encroaching, and the prospect that all this would eventually eat us all up financially.

At first the realization of what it was that was troubling my soul was only vaguely apparent to me. Slowly on the realization of the sense of being orphaned from God began to surface as a conscious awareness. Then one day, while driving to a meeting in Ann Arbor, it all seemed very clear. I had lost the sense of the presence of the divine spirit. That was a jarring confrontation with reality, starkly set in bold relief in my mind. It felt clarifying to sense that the insight rang true to what I was feeling in my heart. God was out of touch just when I felt I needed most the intimations of the spirit, to handle if not to make sense out of what was happening to Brenda and the way it was devastating all of the family. I remember thinking then that life is what happens to you when you are busy making other plans.

Though these clarifying intimations were illuminating, they did not decrease the sense of the distance God had moved away—out of my daily life. However, they did give me a sense that I was not going crazy, that I was being coherent and rational about what we were up against as a family, and what we were doing to help Brenda. If I had to go on without God, I would simply need to do that with courage and vigor. That night I slept soundly for the first time in a long time.

Because I suffer from a significant long-standing heart ailment, I usually sleep on my left side so I can breathe properly at night. My right hand lies on top of the blankets. Sometime, well into the depths of the night I was awakened by a sturdy tapping on the back of my exposed right hand. Tap, tap, tap, three times, and not just a light touch—a sturdy tap intending to awaken me! I remember feeling in my vague twilight of sleep, that my wife was trying to awaken me. Just as I was fading back into sleep I felt the tapping again. This time more strongly! Tap, tap, tap, exactly three times, insistently! So finally I cracked open my right eye to see who was there.

No one was there; but right straight out before me, through the window, completely visible just the way I had been lying asleep, I saw the most amazing scene. There, framed perfectly by the window casing, was a perfect picture in the night sky, a picture any astronomer would give his right arm to capture. There hung the brilliant sickle of a quarter moon, with Jupiter, and Saturn perfectly aligned. No artist could have crafted the sight with more aesthetic magnificence. Immediately I was infused with a pervasive sense of utter peace and assurance. It was clearly a moment of the spirit's intimation that despite the distracting difficulties of our lives just then, God's presence was certain and the spirit's ministry was dependable.

The illumination I received was an act of the spirit manifesting in my world of perception in a definitively healing way just at the moment of my need. Moreover, the affect upon my life and spirit was not a result of any correct or obedient response that I had to the vision through the window or the tapping alert on the back of my hand. Indeed, it was not the result of any response on my part at all. Rather it was the case that in the instant I saw the celestial view I also felt infused with an immense sense of peace. The two aspects were one expression of the same presence. It had nothing whatsoever to do with any wish, initiative, action, or response from me in that moment. The total experience of seeing and sensing the infusion of wholeness and wellbeing was instantaneous—a gift from somewhere and someone outside of myself and apart from any dynamics generated by my own spirit, mind, desire, or will.

On the 15th of November, 2008 I completed a six and half year Interim Ministry in a Presbyterian congregation in the suburbs of Detroit, Michigan. Six and a half years is an unusually long time for an interim minister to remain in a congregation. It is more common for this transitional phase of a congregation's life to last about two years. The needs of this particular congregation demanded a longer tenure in preparation for the arrival of a permanent pastor. At the end of four years of work in this church, I felt that very little had been accomplished to heal the wounds and conflicts of this congregation. So on Pentecost Sunday in 2006 I preached a sermon on the passage in Acts 2 that tells the story of the original Pentecost experience the Christian community had with the presence and power of the divine spirit in its daily life. After teasing out the poetry and metaphors of that narrative in the New Testament, I closed with the question, "What would it look like if the Spirit of God blew through this church like a mighty wind and a flaming fire?

I followed this vital question with asking the congregation to join me in the rest of my months or years of ministry there in focusing specifically upon the presence of the divine spirit in our lives. I urged that we endeavor to discern the tangible ways in which we could identify experiences of the presence and work of the Holy Spirit in our personal lives and our congregational life. In subsequent weeks I promised that I would preach on the biblical narratives about the spirit of God operating in the world and I would lead discussion groups focused upon the Holy Spirit, for an hour before and an hour after the worship service every Sunday.

We covenanted together to engage ourselves in that endeavor. In the discussion groups we discussed my sermons on the Holy Spirit and we shared together personal reports on how each of us had sensed the presence and leading or influence of the spirit during the previous week. When I started this series of sermons and discussion groups I feared that there would be little interest and there would be no one sharing stories. Nothing was further from the truth. The groups were well attended, dynamic, and intensely earnest, as there proved to be more life-changing stories to tell than there was time to share them. Everyone who attended had numerous paranormal experiences to report from their personal histories and their daily lives.

I was enormously gratified to see the congregational members spontaneously sharing with each other outside the discussion groups, events that we began to call "moments of the spirit." A wave of new language swept across the congregation in the variety of expressions coined by the members to describe or define their experiences as a moment of the divine spirit. A remarkable new sense of spiritual freedom took over the congregation and it changed the church. I asked them to cultivate a culture of the holy spirit in the church by continuing to notice such special experiences when they happened, naming them as moments of the spirit, sharing the stories with others, keeping track of them, and so developing a sense in ourselves and in the fellowship that the manifestations of the divine spirit were the matrix in which each of us lived, and moved, and had our being as persons and as church.

Almost everybody has these life-changing paranormal experiences of the actions of the spirit in their lives. Almost nobody keeps track of them and even fewer share them with anyone. The reason for this is the same as the reason that the church moved away from focus on the Holy Spirit right from the beginning of Christendom. The experiences of the divine spirit's movement in our lives, is often difficult to discern clearly. It is difficult to be confidently sure of them as authentic events of the spirit. Moreover, those of us who are unfamiliar of what is really happening to us in these paranormal experiences, feel somewhat afraid to tell anyone for fear that they will think us a bit strange. Each of us in turn is waiting for the other person to tell such a story and then we feel free to share our strangely disconcerting, but life-changing, paranormal moments.

It is really quite astonishing that the church, for 17 centuries, has essentially ruled the Holy Spirit out of the church's life, as Tertullian declared so long ago. In John 14 Jesus declared unequivocally that he was departing, the era of God's presence in the world in Jesus was at an end, and the presence of God from then on (about 30 CE?) would manifest itself as Holy or Divine Spirit. Jesus said that spirit would lead us into all the truth about him and about life, if we were open to it and allowed it to do so. Jesus urged that we wait for the spirit, listen with hearing ears to the intimations of the spirit, and share the illuminations of the spirit with each other. That spirit, Jesus said, "Blows wherever it wishes to blow, you cannot see it, but you can hear its voice, see its effects, and celebrate the consequences of its presence."

The difficulty the church had from the beginning with being a Holy Spirit-focused church, lay exactly in that nature of the divine spirit that Jesus mentioned. That is to say, you cannot control the spirit. You can easily control the church's developing doctrines about Jesus, the Christ. The church turned Jesus into a set of theological propositions, canned them in rational definitions, and then declared that the church members were only permitted to consume and digest this canned food for their spiritual nourishment. That resulted in a church that was oriented on the propositional constructs of Christology, which could be controlled and used as the measure of whether anyone was a true believer and a good Christian.

The church stopped looking for, waiting upon, identifying the moments of, or believing in the divine spirit. It was not the spirit that was expected to lead the church. That would be dangerous, running the great risk of chaos and too much variety of faith and opinion, all derived from the unpredictable events of the spirit of God. It was much easier to maintain control and keep the natives quiet, that is, to keep the members obedient, if the work of the spirit were replaced with the authority of the Bishops and the weapon of Christological Orthodoxy. So the church essentially forgot about the divine spirit in the church and neglected Jesus departing words.

Returning the focus of my church to the spirit as the central concern, radically changed and renewed the congregation. Jesus Christ is the church's best memory. The divine spirit is the form of God's presence in this age of the church. That is why the ancient creeds are correct when they lead us to say, "I believe in the Holy Spirit, that is made up of the life and labor of the Holy Universal Church, the communion of the believers, the forgiveness of sins, and our resurrection to eternal life." Had we taken those lines from the creeds as seriously as we should, we would not have lost sight of the presence, power, and providential work of the divine spirit in our experience every day.

In the recent issue of *Books and Culture, A Christian Review*,[1] the issue of spiritual experience is the subject of Christian Smith's review and analysis of a recent book by Ann Taves entitled, *Religious Experience Reconsidered*.[2] Commenting on that book Smith raises the question that

---

1. Christian Smith, Are You Experienced? in *Books and Culture, A Christian Review*, Vol. 16, No. 3, May/Jun 2010, 14–15.

2. Ann Taves, *Religious Experience Reconsidered, A Building Block Approach to*

I have raised repeatedly in this chapter, and in a larger sense, throughout this volume. Smith is the director of the Center for the Study of Religion and Society at Notre Dame, so he is a person who knows a thing or two about spirituality and is not afraid to talk about it. He brings to bear upon the matter of human spirituality the works of the patriarchs in the field, Rudolf Otto, Ninian Smart, and Mircea Eliade.

In his opening questions, Smith echoes the essence of Taves' concern. She seeks to find out what we are talking about. What is religious experience and what do religious experiences tell us about the nature, meaning, and reality of things religious, divine, spiritual, or sacred? Taves wants to know if the multiplicity of paranormal experiences are real, in view of the fact that both secular and religious people report having them frequently everywhere in the world. Even secular folks report these experiences as so profoundly life-changing as to properly be called religious in nature—experiences with the transcendent world or spirit. What is their source, Taves asks, and how are we to make sense of them?

Of course, this is not a new question with Ann Taves or with this present volume. Scholars and non-scholars, alike, have been asking these questions since very ancient times, probably since humans first stepped out upon this planet. Everyone asks these questions. This is not a special domain of psychologists, anthropologists, or professors of religion. In this long time of asking the crucial questions, Taves fears we have gotten very few good answers and Christian Smith agrees with her. Smith points out that during the middle years of the last century there was a lot of talk about religious experiences being nothing but another human experience that comes up out of our psychological natures, wholly explainable as sensations we generate naturally from inside ourselves.

Mircea Eliade and Ninian Smart were famous university professors in their day and tended to take that approach. They tried to rationalize the suggestions that William James had made in his notable Gifford Lectures (1902), published as *The Varieties of Religious Experiences* a hundred years ago.[3] James thought all paranormal experiences should be taken seriously for exactly what they seemed to be, namely, authentic

---

the Study of Religion and Other Special Things (Princeton: Princeton University Press, 2009).

3. William James, *The Varieties of Religious Experience* (New York: The New American Library, Mentor Books, 1958).

religious experiences. *In the end*, as Taves and Smith observe, Eliade and Smart agreed that such experiences tended to occur in the domain of religiosity and so should be considered to be sacred, transcendent, and perhaps mythical and magical.

James noticed that such experiences followed fairly similar patterns in the experience of all humans regardless of their cultural or social setting. In every case, James thought, these experiences were human encounters with the divine spirit as that person understood or named the spirit of God. He wanted to allow those existential experiences to stand as they were reported by persons who experienced them. He noted that the importance of those religious experiences lay in the fact that they were such dramatically constructive life-changing events. That certified them as authentic spiritual processes so far as James was concerned.

Rudolf Otto emphasized the fact that such experiences were our "sense of the presence of that which is Holy."[4] Friedrich Schleiermacher had made the same point two centuries ago (1812), calling them the human experiences of the numinous.[5] Both Otto and Schleiermacher meant that such a numinous experience is a spiritual or otherworldly sense of knowing, which Schleiermacher felt always involved a feeling of utter dependence upon God. Eliade and Smart also thought the term, numinous, was a good description of what humans apparently experience in these "moments of the spirit."[6]

There have always been scholars who wished to reduce these numinous moments of divine encounter to some empirically scientific and earth-bound explanation. However, the more study that was invested in this matter during the 20th century, the more the focus tended to shift toward a post-modern acknowledgment that the life-changing paranormal experiences people have are simply not accounted for in terms of humanistic equations of the sciences that allow only for the truth we can gain through the five material senses. That empiricism simply did not work for this arena of investigation. So that kind of science gave way to what we call phenomenological science and heuristic argumentation.

4. Rudolf Otto, *The Idea of the Holy* (New York: Oxford University Press, 1958).

5. Friedrich D. E. Schleiermacher, *Die Praktische Theologie nach den Grundsäzen der evangelischen Kirche* (herausgegeben von Jacob Frerichs) (Berlin: De Gruyter, 1983). See also Schleiermacher, *Glaubenslehre* (Berlin: Frierics, 1830/31).

6. Mircea Eliade, *Cosmos and History, The Myth of the Eternal Return* (New York: Harper and Row, 1959); and Ninian Smart, *The Religious Experience of Mankind* (New York: Scribner, 1969).

Phenomenological science is investigation that simply takes into account all the reports one can get about a certain kind of happening or experience—a collection of the phenomena describing that happening or experience. If you can get a very great amount of such reported data, it may be assumed, you will be able to make some sense out of the patterns and categories that show up in it and then you can draw valid scientific conclusions from all that data. Moreover, heuristic argument means the process by which one takes all that phenomenological data and shows how it fits into discernable patterns that strongly suggest specific causes and effects at work there, as well as the nature and meaning of the data. That is, you do not need to be able to weigh the data in the laboratory or measure it with a meter stick or analyze its chemical make up in order to have solid science on the subject phenomenologically studied and heuristically analyzed.

Even though William James suggested this new way of looking at things more than one hundred years ago, it came into its own as a trusted scientific method in the last third of the last century. It has proven to be an important way to study normal religious experiences worldwide. Now, in the 21st century, the time has come to apply such phenomenological scientific methods to the study of the paranormal religious experiences—the moments of the spirit that humans universally encounter.

Of course, there are those today who wish to throw out this entire line of thought and claim that the "moments of the spirit" are nothing but special and probably pathological events of a psychological nature in the stressed inner functions of human psyches. Such folk argue that the paranormal experiences have no inherent reality and certainly have nothing to do with any encounter with the divine spirit in the world, much less any sort of transcendental experience of "an other world" or of God. Since the rush of French Existentialist philosophy into the American university system after WW II, there was a concerted effort to remove from the university and college curricula, at many institutions of higher learning, all courses and traces of Christianity. Every religion in the world might be taught, except Christianity.

This gave lazy professors, who were more interested in being student-celebrated dilettantes than careful teachers, the freedom to rant and rave about their private philosophies rather address the hard work of careful and honest thought. This has produced an anti-establishment tone to American culture, as a result of which the carefully woven fabric of social ethics and responsible life has virtually come apart at the seams for a host of thoughtless folks.

When the storm of arrogant ignorance will have blown over it will still be necessary to deal with the reality of real paranormal human experiences and account in a responsible way for the life-changing effects of the breakthrough moments of the divine spirit in human life. There are signs of hope. In the last fifteen years we have succeeded in establishing at the University of Michigan the Michigan Center for Early Christian Studies (MCECS). We offer a concentration in Christian Studies in the Department of Near Eastern Studies, which is equivalent to the concentrations in Judaic Studies, Islamic Studies, Buddhist Studies, and the like. Over 50 courses in Christian Studies are now offered to our students at the University of Michigan.

We have 20,000 or more students at the University of Michigan who derive from committed Christian families who take their faith seriously and for whom it shapes their lives. For the first time in history those students are being offered an opportunity to explore in a carefully scientific manner, the rich resources of their own religious heritage. This will surely enhance the likelihood that when these young folks have their paranormal moments of the divine spirit, they will have some clue as to what is happening to them, how to name it and understand it, and why to keep track of those events. They will realize the importance of taking their experiences seriously for what they are, as they stand, thus cultivating a culture of the divine spirit as a constructive life-shaping force in their lives.

The university matches the funds that the MCECS raises to support this program. As we acquire major donors to expand this program to the point of endowing six or seven chairs devoted to Christian Studies, presumably we will be able to provide Majors and Minors in Christian Studies, and eventually a graduate degree matriculation in our field. This is a way of taking seriously the breakthrough events of our encounters with the divine spirit in this world and putting the life-changing empowerment that brings to those who experience it, to work in enhancing the universal human awareness of the meaning of such events in all our lives.

This is an important development to be happening at a number of universities as the 21st century is launching itself. Taves' book gives some energy and affirmation to this process. She is certain that we should take the reports of paranormal experiences seriously and acknowledge the appropriateness of most folks who experience them describing them as religious events. As Smith assesses her proposal, Taves takes seriously how people describe their paranormal and normal religious experiences. Then she carefully examines the mysterious world of human consciousness, what we know about the function of the unconscious, tangible experiences such as dreams, casual attributions, neuroscience in relation to psychology, spiritual conversions, and differences between being religious (spiritual) and following a religion. She assesses how we can get at understanding and interpreting the meaning of all these facets of our potential experiences with the divine spirit.

Taves and Smith reinforce the entire theme of this chapter—indeed, of this book—by settling finally on the fundamental principles I have developed here regarding the special kinds of religious experiences with which this volume deals. First, it is crucial to take such human experiences seriously as they stand and neither dismiss them nor reduce them to mere flukes of human consciousness or psychopathology. Second, our discussion must always be against the background of the important question, "How, when, where, and why, may we honestly anticipate the intimations and illuminations of the Holy Spirit to come to us?" Third, the answer is that the spirit blows where it will and is wholly unpredictable as to whom it visits and in what circumstance or by what means. Fourth, it is crucial to discern the spirits to see if the events are authentic, in order to avoid false attribution and idolatry. Fifth, the watershed criterion is simple in such discernment. If the experience is constructively life-changing it is of the spirit, if not, it is not.

8

The Presence

I HAVE A CLOSE friend who, as a teenage girl, was kidnapped by a criminal gang and held in sexual slavery in an abandoned warehouse for a number of years. She was not alone. There was a small company of girls who had been similarly kidnapped and were likewise held in bondage. They were all deployed for prostitution as a source of income for the criminals who held them. Life for these women was brutal. They were frequently raped by the members of the gang. The leader of the gang was especially sadistic, regularly raping and otherwise abusing both the male members of his mob, as well as the women they held for prostitution. This was invariably intentionally staged and carried out with the entire gang and the company of the women as audience. His violence upon them all was his means of intimidation and control to keep the entire company under his unquestioning command. Such lethal treatment of gang members and prostitutes, alike, continued throughout the years that my friend was imprisoned by these genuinely evil men.

Eventually, during one of the leader's particularly evil rampages, he shot two members of the gang to death in cold blood. In the presence of the women and three or four of his henchmen he blew their brains out with a pistol at close range. Three of the women were also pistol whipped and otherwise brutalized, certain that they too were marked for execution. That evening one of the more sensitive members of the gang grabbed my friend, flagged down a taxi, and rushed her off to a distant part of the city. There he gave her a large envelope full of cash and put her in a house where he said she would be safe. He told her to use the money to get her life on a new and better track.

The most remarkable thing about her report on the years of her enslavement and brutalization was the fact that she felt a constant protective presence with her most of the time. This was always particularly true during the worst crises of abuse, particularly that last day when years of mayhem and insanity on the part of the gang leader seemed to come to an epitome of bloody violence. She had never been a particularly spiritual or spiritually informed person. Yet she found herself constantly reaching out to God for care and rescue in her own silent way, hardly knowing what it was she longed for or asked for except protection and deliverance from a life that had long since come to feel hopeless and helpless.

God came to her, protected and sustained her, and delivered her. She took literally the advice of that captor who set her free. He seemed to have been moved by some inscrutable change of motive and mood on that last evening, and rushed her away to freedom. She often wonders whether he was an undercover agent within that mob, since soon after her deliverance they were all brought to trial. She is now a minister who serves those who are particularly needy and neglected by our society. Like Jesus, himself, she cares most for those for whom others seem to care least. She says that she looked the palpably personified evil of this world squarely in the face. She saw it at its incarnated worst and most brutally sadistic. She now knows it when she sees it, can see it coming afar off, and refuses to turn aside from it with a blind eye, as so often does the rest of society.

This persistence of a sense of The Presence is not an uncommon human experience. It is regularly reported by persons who have come through periods or experiences of utter extremity—times of hopelessness, helplessness, impossible danger, and despair. These events are usually remarkably tangible and palpable experiences of the literal presence of a sustaining and protecting person standing beside one or frequently walking just a bit behind oneself. The presence is usually sensed as so real that one expects to turn around and meet that person standing there or walking along.[1]

When I went off to college there was little money available and so whenever I went home for a weekend or holiday, I hitchhiked the 100 miles up Highway 131. I was a rather slightly-built and small person for my 17 years. I usually had good success in getting rides. On one such journey I was picked up by a gentleman who worked at the Johnson

---

1. The full text of this personal story has been published in Virginia Ingram, Evil Experienced by One Who Was There, Vol. 1, *Definitions, History, and Development*, Ch. 4, in J. Harold Ellens, ed., *Explaining Evil*, 3 vols. (Westport, CT: Praeger, 2011).

Furniture Factory in Grand Rapids, Michigan. He was a very pleasant conversationalist for about 50 miles. Then he began to make a number of moves which seemed very strange to me in my 1940s naivete. It turned out that he was intent upon forcing me into sexual activity with him.

When I became aware of what he was up to, I slid over to the far door of the car. That was not the solution for he said he was going to turn off the highway at the next intersection because he knew of a nice park where we could have some private fun. On the one hand, I knew I was in serious danger. I determined at the first chance to jump from the car. On the other hand, I felt a calm sense of being protected by a steadying force I did not understand. As we approached the traffic light in the center of Reed City mere minutes later, his front tire exploded with a thunderous echo and his car jerked off the road into a parking meter. He cursed, and then said, "Oh that's too bad." I heard nothing further. I ran through the town and escaped. I was delivered.

Suedfeld and Geiger have addressed this issue of a protecting presence sensed by people in situations of extremity.[2]

> People sometimes sense, see, or hear another being in situations in which the actual presence of another being is highly improbable, if not impossible. Psychologists refer to this as the "sensed presence experience." Sensed presence experiences occur in a wide variety of situations, to a wide variety of people, and the presences themselves vary in appearance, identity, and behavior. There are many kinds of sensed presence phenomena. They include ... angelic and other religious visitations, ... "corner of the eye" glimpses of someone almost seen or almost heard ... vivid dreams and daydreams ... experiences ... reported by people in extreme and unusual environments ... of interest ... because no obvious explanation presents itself.[3]

Such sensed presences seem most common in situations in which a person is spent from exhaustion, severe illness, or approaching death.

Many things may be said about these experiences because the reports on such events are numerous and fall into very similar patterns of extremity and the sensations that are induced in the persons feeling the

---

2. Peter Suedfeld and John Geiger, The Sensed Presence as a Coping Resource in Extreme Environments, Vol. 3, *Parapsychological Perspectives*, in J. Harold Ellens, ed., *Miracles: God, Science, and Psychology in the Paranormal*, 3 vols. (Westport, CT: Praeger, 2008), 1–15.

3. Ibid., 1.

presence. First, this often occurs in a low-stimulus situation when the person feels utterly alone, helpless, and sensorially deprived. The sensed presences are not simply there as companions in the struggle but are actually helpers in handling and triumphing over the suffering, whatever it is. Sometimes the presence offers useful information of a concrete cognitive sort and provides advice as to how one may best take the next action. At other times the presence itself actually takes action "in whatever needs to be done to improve the chances of survival."[4] Suedfeld and Geiger offer fifty-eight narratives reporting recorded cases of the experience of such redemptive "apparitions."

> The sensed presence often occurs in the wilderness, mountains, ice fields, jungles, or the ocean. The experience has also been encountered underwater by divers and aloft by pilots and astronauts. Other cases have been reported by survivors of man-made conflagrations, such as the September 11, 2001, terrorist attacks on the World Trade Center, and by prisoners of war. There are several environmental factors that are common to such situations, despite their obvious difference. One characteristic is a relatively unchanging and homogeneous physical and social stimulus environment. Other relevant factors can include physical privation, such as hunger, thirst, illness or injury; psychological stress, unusual temperatures . . . and a perception of danger.[5]

Of thirty-three Spanish mountain climbers studied, 33% experienced the sensation of an accompanying presence behind their own bodies, aiding them in their struggle with extreme circumstances. Frank Smythe came within a short distance from the top of Mount Everest, climbing by himself in 1933. He felt like an unseen companion was assisting him in this extremely difficult ascent and near the summit urged him that he had reached his limit of his high altitude endurance and should turn back. He said that the sense of the presence was so strong that he felt none of the loneliness he thinks in retrospect he would have felt had he been alone.

Smyth reported that he felt like he was tied to his numinous companion by a rope and that if he slipped or fell the companion would save him. So real was this sense of the companion that at one point when he had stopped for a snack, he pulled out a chocolate bar, broke it in half,

---

4. Ibid., 2.
5. Ibid., 2

and turned to give a piece to his companion. He was astonished that no one was there. His companion stayed with him until he reached the base camp where other humans were present. Then he felt very lonely.

Similarly, Maurice Wilson, a bit of a mystic, undertook the Everest climb in 1934. The project was apparently not well planned or equipped. He was not an experienced climber and felt his religious faith would get him through to see the top of the world. While he died in the ill-fated process, his diary was recovered and tells us much. As he lay snow-blinded and suffering from altitude sickness, he felt that someone was with him in his tent the entire time. This afforded him a peace and consolation that apparently saw him through to his death.

I have already noted in this volume that when my grandmother was on her death bed, she saw and spoke to my grandfather who had predeceased her by a decade or so, and who had apparently come to meet her and take her home. Immediately she drew her last breath with a wide smile on her face, and then she was gone. A dear friend in my last congregation suffered for two years from abdominal cancer. As he lost weight and tried to endure the chemotherapy he was consistently gracious and hopeful of his release. During the last days of his life he frequently mentioned to his wife that he saw his parents awaiting him, and he spoke with them on some occasions as though they were present with him in the room. The screen between heaven and earth is more permeable than we usually experience it to be or think it is. The presence of the divine spirit and of the spirits of those we love and cherish is closer than a friend.

These examples of communication with heavenly beings that I have personally experienced in those close to me, ring exactly true to the numerous reports in the near-death research that has been extensively published since Moody's work twenty years ago.

As I noted above, the factors in all the near-death experiences that are reported in the research literature now, involve five or six elements that characterized the experiences and were common to all of them. These factors included the experience that while the person involved was enduring the ordeal of passing from life into death, helper visitors from the "other side" came to meet him or her and provided instructions, consolation, companionship, and a sense of utter peace.

Real life stories abound in the psychological literature, reporting mountain climbers who have all had virtually the same experience of the presence as Smyth and Wilson did.[6] In 1950 Maurice Herzog led a team up Annapurna. As they approached the summit through heavy weather and altitude distress he told his partner that he heard someone else following them. He wanted to call out to his companion but found that he could not do so. He looked around to see the unknown climber. While he saw no one, the sense of his presence persisted until the weather brightened and they returned to base camp.

When Doug Scott and Dougal Haston climbed to the top of Everest on September 24, 1975, they arrived at the summit at 18:00 hours, early evening. It had been a fourteen hour climb up from the camp and it was now too late to return. After dropping down about 500 feet a thickly clouded night fell, hiding the moon. Forced to spend the night, they dug a secure cave in the snow but soon ran out of oxygen. With no food and a quickly exhausted butane heater, they were in dire straights by midnight. It then became a desperate matter of survival. They reported that a third person was sharing the snow hole all night with them, suggesting various actions to enhance survival and even warming them with his own body heat.

A truly notable climber, Reinhold Messner, on a par perhaps with Sir Edmund Hillary, climbed both Nanga Parbat and Everest and in both climbs received psychological help from a sensed presence who was welcome company and helped him handle the loneliness. He recorded one of these experiences while it was happening, saying into the recorder, "I am holding a conversation with someone who is sitting at my side. Is it human? It seems there is another presence besides my own. That is all I can say. It isn't just a voice I hear, I actually sense a physical presence." Jerzy Kukuczka climbed Makalu, 14 miles from Everest, in October 1981. With two fellow climbers he attempted the West Face but had to turn back, so alone he determined to move up the North-West Ridge instead. Encountering a hard wind at 30,000 feet, he set up camp and, exhausted, began to make tea, when he realized that he had company. He experienced the inexplicable feeling that he was not alone. He had an overpowering need to talk to his visitor. The next day he fought on through worsening weather, finding himself periodically stopping to let his visitor catch up. "From time to time I let him pass, so that he could go ahead."[7]

6. Ibid., 2–5.
7. Ibid., 5.

Michael Groom found himself in severe distress in 1987, unable to breathe properly as he lay in his tent, high on the side of Kangchenjunga. Then he felt a presence in the tent next to him. The visitor knelt by his side, lifted him to a sitting position, helped him place his head between his knees so as to breathe more freely. Michael felt the visitor watching over him as long as he was in that situation. At 27,000 feet on Everest in 1994, Steve Swenson was forced by weather and ill-health to recuperate for two days. During the night a woman came to him and urged him to stay awake all night lest sleep bring death in the extreme cold. Later a jolly sort of Sikh man visited him and urged him to descend as rapidly as possible the next day. As he did so a third visitor helped him down. "These characters were very real, and I was taking their advice." When he reached base camp he observed that everything the visitors had instructed him to do were "exactly what I needed to do" to survive.[8]

It is not only in the rarefied atmosphere of high mountains where the visiting presences manifest themselves to persons in special circumstances of urgent need. In 1895 Joshua Slocum sailed alone around the globe, the first to succeed in such a feat. Off the Azores he got food poisoning while fighting a life threatening storm. When he collapsed at the wheel he was visited by a "strange guest," who promised that he was there to assist him and he should lie quietly while his guest took the wheel and manned the sails through the night. He had been reading Columbus' story and was sure the visitor was the master of the Pinta, a seaman of vast experience. When he regained some degree of normalcy and could again take the wheel, he found his small ship on the correct course for his charted destination of Gibraltar. The same strange guest reappeared on numerous occasions during his circumnavigation of the planet.

Enzio Türa, lost for a month in the Indian Ocean without adequate supplies, Dr. Hannes Lindemann in his solo crossing of the Atlantic in 1956 to test whether psychological self mastery can get one through extreme danger, Dr David Lewis sailing alone near the Grand Banks on a Lindemann-type experiment, and Robert Manry who crossed the Atlantic alone in the mid 1960s, all told essentially the same story. In their extremity a helpful visitor appeared with whom they could converse aloud or through some miraculous direct brain to brain communication. Frequently they all experienced a presence taking control of the ship and delivering them from situations of extreme danger.

8. Idem.

Suedveld and Geiger draw their narratives of mountain climbers and sea voyagers to a close with yet another narrative and observation.

> In another case, a woman drifting in a dinghy on the Pacific Ocean told her five companions that during a heavy storm, she had counted seven people in the boat and that a presence behind her had helped them to fight the storm. In their study of survival at sea, E.C.B. Lee and Kenneth Lee wrote of the experiences as being common: "There are many instances where survivors have felt an Unseen Presence, helping and comforting them."[9]

Sir Ernest Shackleton rescued his marooned polar exploration party in 1914–17 by enduring, with two companions, the arduous and life threatening ordeal of climbing over the South Georgia mountains to get help. All reported independently, after the rescue, that during the days when they faced death moment by moment they were sustained and motivated by a visitation from some ethereal realm. Similarly Alan Parker was building temporary shelters for scientific work on Macquarie Island in the Antarctica when a storm isolated and disoriented him and he lost contact with the base camp. At the height of his fear and danger he realized he was accompanied by someone who communicated to him that he should not worry but keep on trying to find his way. Another explorer of the South Pole, Peter Hillary recognized his ethereal visitor as his deceased mother.

Charles Lindbergh said that on his historic solo flight across the Atlantic ethereal visitors were coming and going in his plane cockpit, encouraging him to endure and giving him direction and navigational advice. When Will Jimeno, a police officer, was trapped in the ruins of the World Trade Center Towers, he was injured and after 10 or 12 hours, dehydrated. Then he saw Jesus come to him with a bottle of cold water and his spirits lifted and he had a deep sense of assurance that he would survive. Aron Ralsten was hiking in a Utah canyon when he was trapped by a falling rock, from which he could extract himself only by breaking his arm and cutting it off with a jack knife. He hiked 6 miles with tourniquets and sling made from his torn shirt. He reported to his rescuers that when he had resigned himself to death a young boy came to help him. He talked to him, touched him, carried the boy for a while on his

---

9. E.C.B. Lee and J. E. Elder, *Safety and Survival at Sea* (New York: Giniger-Norton, 2003), 203.

shoulder, and experienced him as a real presence. Some years later he identified the visitor as his future son.[10]

These paranormal experiences have been variously explained as spiritual and supernatural, psychological and natural, or neurological and biochemical phenomena. There is a great danger that reducing them merely to the latter two of those three is the kind of unscientific reductionism that leads away from the truth. It is most likely that the truth is all three of those explanations together, and probably a lot more we do not yet perceive. The divine spirit employs all the channels and potentials of the human organism and probably the organism of this dynamic living planet, to accomplish its illuminating and even rescuing redemptive acts.

There is little reason, it seems to me, to reduce the significance of these events or rewrite them differently than they were experienced. Reductionism is always the direction toward error in a number of ways. It makes our personal or communal biases the determinative principal of interpretation. It erases the relevance of all those parts of the data that do not fit the reductionist paradigm. It assumes that we know more than we know about the phenomena with which we are dealing. With regard to things we do not understand we should always do four things. First, we should watch and listen very carefully to the reports of the data. Second, we should let the phenomena described stand as they are reported. Third, we should attempt in so far as possible to carry out a friendly analysis of possible explanations. Fourth, reductionism generally overlooks the constructive life-changing effect all these experiences had upon the persons who had them, and that should be assiduously avoided.

Most of the reported events had a spiritual and transcendental character about them for those who experienced the presences. This is true to such an extent that most of the persons involved, secular persons or persons of faith, indicated that the experience was religious in nature. Suedveld and Geiger put it like this.

---

10. These narratives are all presented in greater color and detail, with original sources by Suedveld and Geiger in their chapter on Sensed Presence, in Vol. 1, *Parapsychological Perspectives*, Ch. 1, in J. Harold Ellens, ed., *Miracles: God, Science, and Psychology in the Paranormal*, 3 vols. (Westport, CT: Praeger, 2008), 1–9. Their discussion includes the report of Geiger's interview with Alan Parker regarding his Antarctica experiences in March 1968.

> Because the phenomenon is so striking, and because some of the aspects are not adequately explained by any of the theories, it is clear that the sensed presence experience will continue to intrigue . . . . Above all, perhaps, is the need to understand the dramatic helpfulness of the sensed presence, which includes not only encouragement but also factual information such as navigational directions and, on occasion, physical intervention.[11]

These reports of paranormal experiences are remarkably similar in every dimension and aspect to the visits humans generally have that seem to be the divine spirit providing life-changing intimations and illuminations to ordinary people in the ordinary circumstances of daily life. These experiences of the presence of the divine spirit do not only happen on mountain peaks, when lost at sea, or in danger in the desert. They do not only happen in extreme heat or cold. They happen every day to everyday people in every-day circumstance. Moreover, they are all very much alike. I perceive no essential difference between the reports shared in this chapter and the nature of the life-changing moments that have occurred a dozen extraordinary times to me, affording clear cut illuminations, intimations, and communications that have literally healed my life, giving it meaning and direction. The reports of the presence in this chapter are not unique human experiences. They are virtually the same in the essential aspects as those in other kinds of reports of experience people generally have. These seem more common the more the sails of our lives are set close to the wind of the spirit, so to speak.

There is, of course, one disturbing question about all this. What are we to say about those desperate moments of human need, like the fire that killed my little friend, Esther, when no immediate divine or ethereal intervention seems to have occurred? A corollary of that essential question is a sub-question. What are we to say about the fact that it took two years of virtually total dysfunction and anguish for the presence to arrive in my life and finally deliver me from the tragic consequences of my loss of Esther, a deliverance that finally came by means of a life-changing illumination, setting me on a meaningful and purposeful course of life?

What are we to say of the Arctic explorer with his team of 7 Inuits, and 12 non-Inuits, caught in desperate circumstances when the ice trapped their ship. Eleven of his party died. All of the Inuits and one other person had intense experiences of a saving, helping presence.

---

11. Suedveld and Geiger, Op. Cit., 14.

They said that they felt these were religious events. None of these eight died. We do not know if the others had experiences of a presence before they died. None reported it before death. The survivors, including two children, were completely confident and clear about their experience of being kept alive, psychologically resilient, and well by the presence, the entire time. There seems to be no answer to those questions that humans have been asking since the beginning of time.

The authors who have been so helpful to me in this chapter suggest however, that there are four facts about sensed presences that one must take for face value. First, those events happen to persons who are psychologically normal and highly independent achieving people. Second, they occur most graphically and dramatically in stressful circumstances when the life-endangering conditions are extreme in one way or another, and survival seems to be at stake. Third, they assist persons who experience the presence in their need and effort to survive or succeed. Fourth, critical analyses that attempt to reduce the experiences to their component factors or explain them in terms of common empirical or psychosocial paradigms have not begun to account for any aspect of these experiences. A great deal of analytical assessment still needs to be done before we can say anything more scientific about them than the precise and virtually duplicative language in the reports by the persons who had the experiences. Until further analysis is possible, we must assume that they are exactly what they seem to be: visitations from an ethereal world that wishes goodness and grace to us.[12]

---

12. Suedveld and Geiger, Op. Cit., 13–14.

9

Corollary Bible Stories

WHEN WE TAKE OUR own paranormal experiences seriously as intimations or illuminations of the divine spirit, the biblical stories of special prophetic insight or remarkable discernment are much easier to appreciate for what they really were. Moreover, it is then easy to understand that those biblical narratives are not unique, extraordinary, or different from what continues to happen to us today. The biblical characters who experienced special visitations of the divine spirit were persons who consistently lived their lives with the spiritual sail set close to the wind of the spirit. They were open to illuminations and intimations from God.

Some of the biblical prophet visions were dramatic and some were subtle. Hannah longed for a child she could bring up in the faith and tuned to the divine spirit. She prayed in the tabernacle as though wrestling with God. The moment came when she was sure the spirit was visiting her, and as in the case of the conception of my now twelve year old son, she became aware that God had filled her womb and blessed her with a son. From that day on, Hannah was clear on the presence of the divine spirit in her spirit and life, and that awareness shaped the character and vocation of that boy who became Samuel, the prophet. He is known in the Old Testament as a Seer, because he had an unusual capacity to discern surprising things: he routinely envisioned the messages of God to him in the function of his intuition, extrasensory perception (ESP), and prescience.

As described in chapter 5 above, Julian Jaynes said he thought that the biblical prophets had very active function of their right brains and trusted what they perceived through that capacity.[1] Recall that I observed

---

1. Julian Jaynes, Op. Cit.

there that the right hemisphere of the brain in humans is the organ that acquires meaning from life in terms of emotion, intuition, texture, color, beauty, art, feeling, extrasensory perception, prescience, and relationship. Jaynes argued that those perceptions we acquire in our right brains we objectify as messages coming to us from some external source.

Therefore, it is not difficult to understand that such intimations or illuminations are given us to lead us into new and better understandings of ourselves, of God, and of our destiny. Persons "with eyes to see and ears to hear" acknowledge that such experiences are guidance and counsel channeled to us from God by the presence of the spirit in our spirits. Jaynes has helped us greatly in comprehending this aspect of our cognition—our paranormal ways of knowing—and taking them seriously, even though he was not prepared to affirm that the perceptions of our right brains always came from God.

Hannah discerned that in her grief she was being led to implore God for a child. She knew in her right brain that the spirit had visited her, God had answered her prayer. This was immediately confirmed by her conception of Samuel, whom she dedicated to the ministry of the divine spirit in the world from his youth up. I do not see this experience as differing in any way from numerous of my own, such as the conception of my 12 year old son, and those of which others regularly inform me. The spirit's work in the Bible was not special, magical, or other worldly, but rather the spirit's normal mode of operation. The corollary experiences humans have had ever since, and throughout history, as well as those people are having regularly today, are no less divine or authoritative and life-changing than those of the biblical characters.

The Joseph narrative is a story of rather dramatic prescience in which he foresaw in a numinous dream a destiny that could not have been imagined or conjured up from within the scope of his young life experience. His vision from the divine spirit indicated that eventually all his brothers would be dependent upon him and subordinate to him. Clearly it was an illumination that prepared him for the endurance required during his ordeal of abuse by his brothers, their plot to kill him for what they considered to be his arrogance, his enslavement as a commercial object by the Midianites, and his purchase as a servant by Potiphar. His inspired vision held up through the ordeal and focused in a sufficient sense of purpose and divine assurance that he kept his head, despite being imprisoned by Potiphar when his wife slandered Joseph and impugned his reputation.

He seemed not to have despaired in prison but continued to count on the leading of the spirit so that when his fellow prisoners dreamed disturbing dreams he was insightful enough to make sense of them. His intuition proved correct, resulting in his being called from prison by the Pharaoh to explain the Pharaoh's dreams. His intuitive and prescient capacity to perceive and report the meaning of the national leader's dreams resulted in Joseph, in effect, being promoted to ruling Egypt and saving both its population and his own brothers and extended family from starvation. When his brothers trekked to Egypt to buy food from Joseph's ample storehouses his original prescient dreams came true in remarkable detail.

Biblical scholars and lay readers of the Bible have tended to trivialize such stories as that of Joseph, rather than taking it with any kind of literalness. Presumably that is because the story seems preposterous unless one is willing to see a genuine manifestation of the divine spirit's illumination in this individual person's life experience. It is easy for me to take the core story in Joseph's narrative for face value; because my illumination by the divine spirit, at age seven, was essentially no different than Joseph's prescient perceptions.

That is, I do not accord any special authority or supernatural character to the Hebrew Bible or the New Testament. These are all human books, written by human beings; but it is clear that the Bible is made up of reports by the biblical characters about how their lives were filled with the spirit of God. What makes the Bible God's revelation is that their reports inform us of how people with lives full of God, so to speak, experience the divine spirit in ways that produce constructive life-changing experiences. Those reports, when they are constructive, can be taken for face value as solid testimony regarding how God acted and is acting in history in personal lives—reports by people whose life sails were set close to the breath of God—wind of the spirit.

Abraham is a biblical character whose very historicity is questioned by many. However, such scholars as John Van Seters and others believe we have solid reasons to take Abraham's story as it stands. Raised in the fatalistic polytheism and stinking urban morass of southern Mesopotamia, Abraham imagined that better things were possible for his family and his flocks and herds. He communicated his vision of a better, spirit-led future to his extended family and they all moved with their households and possessions to the apex of the Fertile Crescent in northern Mesopotamia, to a city he founded named Haran, in what is now Syria. Abraham's inner quest was still not quieted. The divine spirit was urging him onward so after some years he moved with his nuclear family south into Palestine. There he pastured his flocks and herds on the mountain sides and the Shepalah that is now the land of Israel.

There one night, gazing at the infinity of the stars of heaven and watching the moon set over the Mediterranean Sea, he received an intense and definitive illumination. His right brain turned on and in it a message spelled out that he immediately sense was a word from the spirit of God. "I will be a God to you and to your children after you, throughout their generations, for an everlasting covenant. You will be my people and I will be your God—no strings attached." In one fell swoop his irksome perplexity about oppressive Chaldean polytheism was resolved. He was suddenly clear about the meaning of life and the meaning and destiny of his life. "Your progeny will be as the stars in the heavens in number, and as the sands upon the sea's shore."

In one spirit-driven illumination Abraham got the entire picture clear in his mind. God is singular, not multiple as in polytheism. God's spirit is pervasive throughout the world—from the starry heavens above to the moral law within. It is as intensely present in the open fields of Palestine as in the sophisticated urban centers in Iraq, where the spirit had first laid hold of him and moved him out to Haran. Moreover, the central point he grasped was that the God whose spirit illuminated him was obviously wholly for him and not against him, inspite of himself. That illumination has shaped the spirituality and destiny of all *authentic* Jews, Christians, and Muslims, who are true to that covenant heritage, ever since Abraham's revelatory moment of the spirit on the hills of Judea.

Why supernaturalize that story? Why make some other worldly narrative of it? That trivializes it. It is just the same kind of thing that is happening to all of us regularly, if we are tuned to the presence of the spirit of God in the world and in our lives. The same may be said for the stories of Moses, Paul, Peter, and Jesus himself.

Moses was certainly well educated by the priests of Egypt, at the time the most educated persons in the world west of China. They had archives which held historical information that went back to prehistory. Their sciences of medicine, hydraulics, architecture, history, philosophy, geometry, architecture, and the like, were remarkably advanced long before the time of Moses. From Moses story we have reason to believe that he was aware of such historical facts as the law codes of the Pharaohs and of Hammurabi of Mesopotamia, who lived 500 years before Moses.

In any case, after Moses had led the Israelites out of Egypt he realized he needed to take steps to form them into an organized society if they were to succeed in setting themselves up in a new land as an independent nation. In his illumination by the divine spirit on or near Mt. Sinai, he experienced the vision of an ordered society shaped by deference to that divine spirit and regulatory contract law. So, the Ten Commandments express both. The first four are contract law to regulate our relationship of awe-filled deference to God. The last six are contract law regulating our relationship with God's world, and our society or other persons.

Moses' spiritual illumination constituted a model in which a society that wishes prosperity and tranquility needs to adhere to this simple set of regulations. If you do not adhere to a social contract against theft, for example, you cannot get any sleep and die of exhaustion. That is, if thievery runs rampant in your world, and you take my TV, you need to stay up all night with your shotgun loaded because you know I am coming for your car. If a society does not have a universal understanding that one should avoid messing with someone else's wife, the society will be destroyed by fear, paranoia, unfaithfulness, violation of trust, and loss of companionship, to say nothing of the destruction of families. Sound familiar? Moses' illumination was fairly important, and obviously of the spirit. We trivialize it to our own personal hurt. Some of us have learned that directly from tragic experience. It is fortunate that in keeping with the vision of Abraham, the spirit of God has a way of entering into our gross errors and using them as media for our growth in sensitivity to the presence of that spirit and its healing graces.

Peter had many special moments of divine visitation and he needed all he could get. However, the most definitive one was probably a dream he had that cracked open, once and for all, his racist notion that God was primarily interested in Jews. He realized how dumb an idea that was when in a deep sleep he saw a container descend from heaven filled with all kinds of non-kosher food. In the dream he heard the divine spirit say, "Peter, take some of this food and eat it." His response was to be horrified and he refused to eat anything non-kosher. At that point the spirit spoke again and said to him, "Peter, what I call clean, do not you deign to call unclean!"

When he awoke, Peter realized that the message meant he should proclaim the Christian message to Gentiles as well as Jews. Within minutes messengers from Cornelius, a Roman Centurion, appeared at his door asking him to baptize that gentile and his entire family. Peter obliged because he perceived that his dream was a prescient revelation from God's spirit through the channel or medium of a dream, preparing him for just this moment and insisting that he perform the baptisms. Preachers have made an extraordinary thing of this narrative for 2000 years, but it is not extraordinary. It is one of the quite ordinary ways in which the illumination of the spirit comes to people who are open to the spirit and awaiting its intimations. Peter's experience is little different from my own life-changing event of the voice awakening me in the night enjoining me aloud to "Trust in the Lord, and do good," rather than worry about the heresy trial and the danger of losing my ordination. Moreover, as in my case, Peter seems to have been immediately delivered from his racism and bad theology. It was just taken away, not because he obeyed the voice, but because the spirit cleansed his spirit, as the spirit cleared my soul spontaneously from any further anguish about my potentially lethal predicament. It was just simply gone.

Paul's special conversion event fits just as simply into this same model of divine illumination. Paul had been on an official commission for some time, perhaps years, to impose the final solution upon all Christian Jews he could find. He was simply slaughtering them. Indeed, he was on one of his journeys to Damascus to exterminate the Jewish-Christian community there. Now Paul was a well educated Pharisee, having studied under the famed teacher, Gamaliel. He also was a Jew who had become acclimatized to Greek culture and was quite enamored of it, as were most Jews by that time.

So Paul was no ignoramus. You can imagine, therefore, that he must have had a lot of internal psychospiritual conflict about being fervent for the cause of God by killing a lot of religious people from his own community. Well, the complexity of it caught up with him psychologically and spirituality and that became the occasion for the breakthrough by the divine spirit. Riding along on his horse, with the company of enforcers whom he commanded, turning his psychospiritual turmoil over in his head and heart, feeling the hot sun on his bald pate, suddenly it was all overwhelming. He lost his orientation, fell off his horse, had some kind of sunstroke or brain fit, in which he heard the voice of the spirit. Jesus was saying to him, "Paul, why are you fighting this losing battle against God?"

That divine illumination radically and constructively changed his life. From a killer he changed into a self-sacrificing promoter of the Jesus movement. From antagonist against the Christian cause he became its chief protagonist. In that illumination of the spirit on the Damascus road Paul seems to have gotten the whole story just the right way around. He virtually singlehandedly carried the cause across the Mediterranean world. Paul made Christianity what it is supposed to have been ever since, a new kind of spirituality centered in a God of radically unconditional grace and of universal salvation.

Was Paul's life change or the spirit's manifestation in it remarkably different from yours and mine? Were the moments of the spirit in the Bible different from ours in the 21st century? Not in the least, so far as I can see. Folks have considered the biblical narratives unique only because humanity has lost track of our own daily experiences of the spirit's ministry. We were dissuaded from taking our spirit intimations seriously because in the fourth century the official church decided that only the voice of the bishops could be considered the voice of God to us. That proved to be a great tragedy wreaked upon the church for the sake of according all authority to the hierarchy. It sheared from the lives and spirits of ordinary Christians the freedom and redemption that comes from living life with the ear tuned to the intimations of the spirit every day. The bishops talked the Christian laity out of setting their spiritual sails close to the wind of the spirit and out of trusting that wind alone to bring them home to God's spirit and will.

Enoch walked with God. At least that is what the early chapters of Genesis tell us. We have no way of discerning who this ancient figure was. Was he a real person or a kind of eponym—a type of typical character needed to fill out a story about some characteristic of the ancient Israelite memory? It makes little difference which of those is the case. What is obvious about Enoch's story is that it was believable to the people who told it and recorded it. For it to be believable, it had to ring true to the sort of experiences people were having. They told the story about Enoch because his story epitomized a type of experience that some people were having, people who were known for having their sail set close to the wind.

There were people they knew who were so tuned to the presence of God's spirit every day of their lives that it became the style of their lives. People said that it was as though they were simply walking around in total God-consciousness all the time. It shaped their lives and they were regularly illumined by the intimations of the spirit of God. Have you known such persons? I have! They are as common today as they ever were, even though the narratives of the Bible seem to hold Enoch up for a deferent awe, as though his spiritual intensity were somehow unusually strong.

David, the king of Israel and Judah a thousand years before the time of Julius Caesar, Caesar Augustus, Philo Judaeus, Josephus, and Jesus, the Christ, was an intensely spiritual person from his youth up. When we read his psalms we realize what a deep sense of the presence of the divine spirit he had already as a shepherd boy tending his father's sheep day and night on the hills of Judea. He observed the starry heavens, the traverse of the rising and setting sun, the drama in the change of weather, and the relationship of all these things to the vitality of life on this planet. He likened the perfect symmetry of the material universe to the order he perceived the divine spirit to be forming in the moral universe (Psalm 19).

During his adolescent and adult years he turned into a brash and often brutal terrorist. After his rise to kingship he continued his deadly aggression as a virtually indiscriminate warrior. Eventually this led to his stealing the wife of one of his best soldiers and murdering her husband to get him out of the way. Life hardened that aesthetically and spiritually sensitive shepherd boy. In his years as king one had to practically hit him over the head with a heavy plank to crack him open again to the inner spiritual core. The spirit moved Nathan the prophet to confront David about his murder and adultery. Nathan hit him straight over the head with a heavy (ethical) weapon, so to speak. That cracked him open and we have from him a profound expression of authentic spirituality. Psalm 51 is his penitent response to his moral failure. He confesses his transgression, pleads for God's mercy, and prays for a clean heart and right spirit.

The spirit of God gave David the experience of a deep sense of forgiveness. Psalm 32 is his grateful testimony to that. "Blessed is the person whose transgression is forgiven, whose sin is blotted out. Blessed is the man whom the Lord charges with no iniquity and whose spirit is cleansed of all inauthenticity." From then on life repeatedly cracked David open with extreme pain: the violation of his daughters, the insurrection of his sons, and the death of his beloved Absalom.

Life seemed almost as brutal to David, in the end, as he had been brutal in his warrior years. These awful wounds in his life became the apertures through which the divine spirit entered his spirit and engendered spiritual insight and sensitivity. How absolutely typical and common this is in human life! Of course, God did not clobber David with these afflictions, though he probably deserved it. However, the spirit of God entered into David's life through these channels and because of it he could write, "The Lord is my shepherd . . . even though I walk through the valley of the shadow of death I will not fear that evil will come upon me there, for the spirit is with me making meaning out of my pain."[2]

Henri Nouwen suggested, in his winsome fashion, that there are only six holes through which the divine spirit can get into the human world: the holes in a broken heart, the holes in the brokenness of the chaotic and conflictual world, the holes in Jesus hands and side, the holes in our inevitable wounding by our failures and losses, and the holes we stab into others by our narcissistic insensitivity. These terrors are the opportunities and channels of the divine spirit to our spirits, Nouwen said.[3] I am sure he is correct that these are some of the vital wind tunnels through which the spirit blows. The spirit comes to us in constructive life-changing modes in every conceivable way we can imagine. The point is, the spirit comes to us! Unsought! Unasked! Wreaking blessing!

Isaiah's story of life-changing experiences of illumination by the divine spirit is particularly dramatic (Isa 6). One day while he was at regular worship in the temple he suddenly saw God present to him there. We call such a thing a theophany. That means simply an experience of seeing God. It was very much like my experience at age 7 when I was illumined

---

2. There are scholarly debates regarding which Psalms should properly be assigned to David, himself, as the author. In this volume those cited as David's psalms are so identified in the RSV and in any case carry within them so much of the tone and content of David's type of confession, implorations, thanksgiving, and praise that one can confidently conclude that they were written at least in his spirit and that if he did not pen them himself, given half a chance, he would have. They are surely Davidic Psalms.

3. Henri J. Nouwen, *The Wounded Healer* (New York: Doubleday—Image Books, 1979).

through and through with a revelation of my destiny for the rest of my life. Isaiah was caught up, as it were, in what seemed to him to be the aura of God's presence. He said that he saw, felt, and heard God's spirit setting him on the road of his divine vocation. The spirit made it plain to his mind and heart that he was to tell everybody who would listen, everything he understood about the unconditional grace of God. It was 740 BCE when Isaiah experienced this illumination by the spirit. Isaiah was a prolific prophet after that day when the spirit inspired him. Moreover, he seems to have founded a school of prophets that continued long after him. They apparently wrote the last third or half of his biblical book

Like many of the biblical characters, Amos was a farm boy from "up north" and he experienced numerous visitations from the spirit of God, as a result of which he had a deep sense of being called to preach. He had the special sense that he was called or driven to preach to the urban communities of his time which had deteriorated to lawless and immoral chaos. Some of the wealthy people were exploitive of others so the rich got richer and the poor got poorer. Indeed, some of them enslaved the poor as indentured servants or people indebted to them somehow, and they were willing to buy and sell the human beings as objects of property. Amos was moved by the divine spirit to cry out that there were people who would sell the righteous for silver and the poor for a pair of alligator boots (Amos 2:6).

Hosea's story of the divine spirit changing his life is even more dramatic than that of Amos and certainly as remarkable as that of Isaiah. The spirit sent him on a very difficult pilgrimage that turned into a metaphor of the way God deals with all of us humans. The spirit intimated to Hosea that he should marry a prostitute and love her into sanity and spiritual health. However, it proved to be virtually impossible. She liked prostitution a lot better than his love. She kept running back to the red light district and setting up shop there, sort of like down-town Amsterdam. The spirit kept on intimating to Hosea that he should take her back and love her until she was healed of her degraded life. So he did, but this repeated itself a large number of times.

Finally, when he took her back she was pregnant, but, of course, not by him. This happened three times in a row. So he named the three children by Hebrew names that meant, in effect, "These are not my kids!" Well, the divine spirit kept at him and finally his wife caught on to his profound love for her and as a result the spirit got into her life and she loved him. Of course, she was probably worn out by then. However, that is beside the point, because the divine spirit can use all sorts of conditions to get into the spirit of a human being. In any case, it changed her life, and Hosea adopted her children as his own, and the family became a blessed and redeemed family. Now the metaphor of God's way of handling all of us in radical, unconditional, universal grace, and forgiveness, becomes evident in the last line of this Hosea story. There the spirit prompts Hosea to blurt out, quite inspite of himself, "Where it was said, 'These are not my kids' it shall be said instead, 'They are sons of the living God!'" That has been the hope and relief and joy of generations of flawed, but spiritually attuned, persons for the last 2600 years!

Marcus Borg describes Jesus in an intriguing way that is probably closer to the truth than most of us have managed to get, in our understanding of that unusual first century man from Nazareth in Galilee. Borg says he was a man with a life full of God.[4] I take that to mean that Jesus was about as intensely conscious of and shaped by the divine spirit as any human being can ever be. Whether one reads Matthew, Mark, and Luke on the one hand, or the quite different Gospel of John on the other, one gets the clear impression that Jesus lived his life wide open to the spirit and with his spiritual sail set very close to the wind of God's breath. Not only do we see him dealing with the deep and ultimate questions of spirituality all the time in his life, but he also had the habit, apparently, of spending plenty of time just concentrating upon or communing with the spirit of God.

However, the gospel testimony has a couple of stories about very special experiences Jesus had of encountering the divine spirit in ways that radically changed his life. When he came out of the northern province of Galilee where he was raised, and went to meet John the Baptist at the Jordan River. John was preaching about spiritual renewal through repentance and divine forgiveness, and baptizing a lot of people who took him seriously. Baptism became a symbol for them of the way the

---

4. A remark made in a lecture by Marcus Borg at the First Presbyterian Church in Ann Arbor Michigan. See also Marcus J. Borg, *The Heart of Christianity, Rediscovering a Life of Faith* (New York: HarperCollins, 2003); Borg, *Meeting Jesus Again For the First Time: The Historical Jesus and the Heart of Contemporary Faith* (New York: HarperCollins, 1994); Borg, *Jesus in Contemporary Scholarship* (Valley Forge: Trinity Press International, 1994); Marcus J. Borg, ed., *Jesus at 2000* (Boulder: Westview Press, Division of HarperCollins, 1997); Marcus J. Borg, *Conflict, Holiness, and Politics in the Teachings of Jesus* (Harrisburg: Trinity Press International, 1984).

divine spirit changed their lives through John's preaching. So Jesus was also baptized by John and in the process had an intense intimation from the spirit of God. He was sure that he heard God speak out loud to him and tell him that he was a son of God that God particularly cherished and about whom God was very pleased.

I would imagine that this moment was a culmination of a long life of intense pursuit of the divine spirit by Jesus, probably from his childhood experience in the temple, when he seemed to have an unusual illumination. In any case, immediately after his baptism Jesus went on a forty day retreat. It is clear that during this time he struggled with understanding the intimations in the theophony he had received from the spirit at the time of his baptism—the "voice from heaven", as it were. This is clear because we see Jesus, in the narrative of his retreat in the solitude of the Judean wilderness, reflecting on three possible meanings of his call to be a son of God.

The gospel reports on his "temptations in the wilderness" indicate that he considered that being the son of God might mean for him the same thing it meant to Alexander the Great. In his wrestling with the intimations of the spirit he considered bowing down to the temptations of power for setting the world on its proper course. (1) Did the voice from heaven mean he should undertake military conquest, gain the political and military prowess to restore the nation of Israel to its independence from the Romans, and reestablish it as a self-governing nation, as in the days of King David or the Maccabees? (2) Did the being a special son of God mean that he should use his special abilities to turn stones into bread and so be able to feed all the hungry and nurture all the poor of the world, thus solving the world's social problems and inequities? Or (3) did the spirit's illumination at his baptism mean that being the son of God meant captivating the world with some spectacular psychological manipulation, jumping from the temple parapet and trusting the angelic host to save him?

After all, many people were called sons of God in those days. Its primary meaning throughout the world of that time was "righteous man." Moreover, Alexander the Great was called the son of God and under that title he conquered the entire then-known world. Jesus apparently actually wondered if that was what the divine spirit was calling him to do—to raise a revolution in Israel and wield the power necessary to revitalize God's people as a community of independent agents to bring about the reign of God in Israel and perhaps in the whole world.

Alternatively, it was surely as true then as now that all the issues of statesmanship and politics were centered in the economy. Was his calling as son of God to institute the kind of economic reform in which the rich and poor could both enjoy the prosperity and peace of God's Shalom? If one started with turning stones to bread and making sure there was no starvation anywhere any more, the whole world would bow at one's feet. On the other hand, televangelists get a long way toward controlling the attitudes of society by psychological manipulation, so perhaps he could too, Jesus apparently ruminated.

So Jesus knew that the spirit was speaking with him and that he was being led into a new and unknown destiny, but he was unclear as to just what the spirit was saying. By the end of his retreat, however, he had figured it out. He discerned that the spirit of God was illumining his spirit with the clear vision that his job as son of God was to be the Son of Man. The concept and title, Son of Man, had a long history in Judaism by the time of Jesus. It referred to the man who came from heaven to reveal the mysteries of God. Those mysteries were not so mysterious, as John's Gospel makes clear. To proclaim the mysteries of heaven meant to tell the world that God's reign of grace-that-works and love-that-heals had begun in Jesus' life and ministry. It included the message that the reign of that divine spirit was happening in the world and would spread all over the world.

The mystery of that love and grace was also very simple, as we see in John's Gospel better than in any of the other three. It simply meant that God had decided before creation that he was going to save the entire world no matter what; that he forgave all sin and iniquity in advance; that all humans are accepted by God inspite of themselves, and that fear, guilt, and shame are not relevant to the equation of our relationship with God. This implied that there was going to be no judgment day, no second coming of Christ, no cataclysmic end of history, no extermination of the wicked and salvation of the righteous. John seems to be the only gospel writer who really caught on to that central message in Jesus' personal illumination by the divine spirit, because that is the picture he paints in his gospel. Paul seems to have seen that too, of course, as the universal salvation in Romans 8 says so clearly.

Jesus obviously wrestled with the divine spirit in his spirit in trying to sort out which of the various options for the renewal of Israel was the one God's spirit was trying to lead him to articulate. In the end he chose the long, inefficient, but redemptive and healing course of teaching that the divine mode is love and grace. His illuminating encounter with the intimations of the divine spirit proved to be a massively life-changing event in his case. It led him down a trajectory what imprinted itself so indelibly upon the contours of history and upon all our minds that all of human life turns on the fulcrum of his vocation ever since. His impact upon us all outstrips by far that of Alexander the Great.

His perceptions of the spirit's presence in his life led him on almost a straight line to a blood-spattered Roman cross on a windswept hill outside a chaotic town in an irrelevant and troublesome province, remote from the center of the significant action in the world. What made that event a metaphor of the divine spirit's message, was the unforgettably horrid spatters of blood from the heart of a rather nice guy from Nazareth, who by that time was hated by every body that counted, because he cared so much for all those for whom others cared very little at all. He counted as precious those whom others were sure did not count.

The intimations of the spirit in his life cost him dearly when he committed himself to following them operationally, without relenting. But the divine spirit was not finished with him there. Those who cared about him saw him again after he had made the transition to the other world. In his glorified state he returned through the veil and manifested himself to them for their reassurance. The screen between this world and the next proved to be surprisingly permeable and their realization of that has become the spirit-formed and spirit-filled hope of humanity.

10

Mystical Spirituality

MYSTICISM HAS BEEN A type of spiritual experience and a source of religious behavior since humans started to look for the sources of meaning in life. Indeed, it is almost certain that people had significant life-changing mystical experiences even before they were able to conceptualize the quest for meaning, or wonder about the nature and function of life in this world. Mysticism is that dimension of spiritual experience that arises within us at a level that is not dependent upon the formulation of thoughts, the intentions of our wills, or even our consciousness of discreet feelings. Nonetheless it gives us an almost indescribably awareness of profoundly meaningful illumination, gratifying intimations, and sublime wellbeing. We feel that we are in the presence of The Holy, or infused with the presence of The Divine.

Humans have testified to such experiences throughout history, and undoubtedly the mythic faith systems that come down from prehistory were formulated mainly from such mystical experiences; or from a life of mystical wonder at the amazing facets and functions of the material world around us and the enspirited world within us. A fine friend of mine, Dan Merkur, is a profound scholar of the matters and mysteries of psychology and the amazing potentials of the human psyche. He recently wrote a book that will last a century in its relevance to the world of psychological scholarship and is particularly relevant to our subject matter in this volume.[1]

---

1. Dan Merkur, *Explorations of the Psychoanalytic Mystics* (Amsterdam and New York: Rodopi, B.V., 2010). Merkur notes that though unknown outside the psychoanalytic profession and virtually ignored within it, a number of notable psychoanalysts may be seen as holding to a mystical perspective. These include, surprisingly, Otto Rank (1884–1939), Erich Fromm (1900–1980), Marion Milner (1900–1998), D. W. Winnicott (1896–1971), Heinz Kohut (1913–1981), Hans N. Loewald (1906–1993), Wilfred R. Bion (1897–1979), and still living, James S. Grotstein, Neville Symington, and Michael

Merkur informs us that these scientific mystics were notable for the fact that they highly valued an expressive mysticism that understands the entire world of physical and psychic reality to be a seamless unity—all of reality a unified system. The expressiveness of this mysticism takes the form of communicating the inner perceptions of the human spirit in externalized forms that others can share. These mystics tended to see the creative capacity of the human spirit as an expression of an interior mystical perception, applied to the physical material of the graphic arts, sculpture, painting, literature, and culture-creation in general.

While mysticism, mystical moments in people's lives, and the experiences of persons who may be identified as mystics, are unique to each individual and each experience, there are numerous similarities throughout the varieties of such religious experience. Merkur notes that Evelyn Underhill believed that "mysticism in its pure form, is . . . the science of union with the Absolute, and nothing else, and . . . the mystic is the person who attains this union."[2]

In a remarkable letter, written to Henry William Rankin on June 16, 1901, between the ninth and tenth of his twenty Gifford lectures, William James summarized his foundational idea.[3]

> In these lectures the ground I am taking is this: The mother sea and fountain head of all religions lies in the mystical experiences of the individual, taking the word mystical in a very wide sense. All theologies and all ecclesiasticisms are secondary growths superimposed; and the [mystical] experiences make such flexible combinations with the intellectual prepossessions of their subjects [theologians or philosophers], that one may almost say that they [mystical experiences] have no proper *intellectual* deliverance of their own, but belong to a region deeper, and more vital and practical than that which the intellectual inhabits. For this they are also indestructible by intellectual arguments and criticisms. I attach the mystical or religious consciousness to the possession [existence in us] of an extended subliminal self with a thin partition through which messages make irruption. We are thus made

---

Eigen. One might even include James Hillman, though Merker does not discuss him as part of the group.

2. Evelyn Underhill, *Mysticism: A study in the nature and development of man's spiritual consciousness*, (New York: New American Library, 1910), 72. See Merkur, Op. Cit., 1.

3. Charles P. Henderson, ed., "Religion in this Way is Absolutely Indestructible," William James on the Gifford Lectures, *Cross Currents*, 2003, Fall, 464–5.

convincingly aware of the presence of a sphere of life larger and more powerful than our usual consciousness, with which the latter [our conscious awareness] is nevertheless continuous. The impressions and impulsions and emotions and excitements which we thence receive help us to live, they found invincible assurances of a world beyond the senses, they melt our hearts and communicate significance and value to everything and make us happy. They do this for the individual who has them, and other individuals follow him. Religion in this way is absolutely indestructible. Philosophy and theology give their conceptual interpretations of this experiential life. The farther margin of the subliminal field being unknown, it can be treated as by Transcendental Idealism, as an Absolute mind with a part of which we coalesce, or by Christian theology, as a distinct deity acting on us. Something not our immediate self, *does* act on our life!

From his work James was able to distill the following judgments.[4] First, the visible world is part of a more spiritual universe from which it draws its chief significance. Second, that union or harmonious relation with that higher order universe is our true end and purpose in life. Third, prayer or inner communion with the spirit of that universe, be that spirit "God" or "law", is a process wherein work is really done, and spiritual energy flows in and produces effects, psychological and material, within the tangible world of real phenomena.

It is important to remind ourselves here of our definition of spirituality, namely the irrepressible inner human quest for meaning. This quest is a function of the *psyche* or *pneuma* and expresses itself in religious behavior. This quest reaches for transcendental meaning and relationship; and for the meaning of relationship with our material world and the persons we encounter within it. James did not make quite the crisp distinction between spirituality and religion that I make, but it is not difficult to discern at each turn of the road, to which of the two he is referring. James' massive collection of phenomenological data provided a broad base for his heuristic conclusion that one of the most tangible evidences for the profound reality of the "moments of the spirit" is the remarkable zest for life they consistently afford those who experience them: a constructive life-change.

---

4. William James, Op. Cit., 367–391. See also Frederick Burkhardt and Fredson Bowers, eds., *The Works of William James, The Varieties of Religious Experience* (Cambridge, MA: Harvard University Press, 1985).

Mystical Spirituality   121

The things regarding spirituality and religion that interested James tended to be those of individual experience, rather than general categories. He was always looking for the experienced reality, not the theoretical concept or unified theory. He acknowledges at the outset that religious fervor and spiritual quest can produce psychological pathology as well as a full sense of wellbeing. He is interested in what makes the difference and how we can tell the difference. He says candidly, "There is no doubt that as a matter of fact a religious life, exclusively pursued, does tend to make the person exceptional and eccentric."[5]

However, in assessing the history of religious traditions, his important emphasis is upon the fact that persons who simply follow conventional religious rituals of any sort, Buddhist, Christian, Jewish, or Muslim, are simply acting out a religious practice made for them by others. James thinks this cannot possibly do much for a person's spiritual quest. "His religion has been made for him by others, communicated to him by tradition, determined to fixed forms by imitation, and retained by habit."[6] James calls this second-hand religion and he has no interest in commenting further upon it. The important thing is the original experiences, the pattern-setting processes that produced the religious traditions we encounter in our own day.

James focuses the issue further by declaring, "These experiences we can only find in individuals for whom religion exists not as a dull habit, but as an acute fever . . .."[7] He suggests that people who are that intense about pursuing their quest for meaning are spiritual geniuses and, as such, are worthy of both commemoration and emulation. They show us the way. Sometimes the nature of their spiritual intimations, insights, vision, perceptions, and experiences seem ethereal or even otherworldly. In any case, an authentic human meaning quest generally requires exalted spiritual and emotional sensitivity and intuitive understanding. James observes that such levels of spiritual experience, which fill one with a sense of connection with God or transcendent understanding, accord a certain aura of authority and influence to the experience itself, and to the testimony of the person who lives on that plain of spiritual awareness, vision, and insight.

5. James, Op. Cit., 24.
6. Idem.
7. Idem.

James challenged those who reduced such authentic, heightened spirituality to mere psychopathology or to the sublimation of sexual forces in our persons and personalities. He insisted that, while certain types of psychotic ideation and behavior are often centered around religious terms, notions, and claims, or other religious material, it is easy to tell the difference between true spirituality and genuine religion, on the one hand, and mental illness, on the other. As Jonathan Edwards had already insisted three centuries before James, in *A Treatise Concerning Religious Affections*,[8] the roots of human spiritual and religious qualities and expressions are much deeper than we can plumb, but true religion is known by its fruitfulness. "Our *practice* is the only sure evidence, even to ourselves, that we are genuinely Christian" (emphasis added).[9] Edwards had put it quite similarly in saying, in effect, that the degree to which our spiritual experience and religious behavior produces good concepts, character, and conduct demonstrates the degree to which it is genuinely spiritual and divine.

Thus, by his challenges of those who take a superficial view of the human hunger for meaning and the spiritual quest it engenders, James once again confirms the importance of his insistence upon an *empirical* approach to understanding the varieties of religious experience. It is in the workable quality of the practical results, produced by a person of superior achievement in the spiritual quest for meaning and religious relevance, that we can establish the firm foundation of certainty regarding the genuiness of his or her spiritual vision or understanding.

Of course, it helps a person in the spiritual quest to be somewhat neurotic. As Karen Horney said so well in her book, *The Neurotic Personality of Our Time*, to be neurotic means to have a slightly or seriously larger sense of anxiety about things, about anything, than reality would warrant.[10] I have said for many years that ministers of the gospel need to be mildly neurotic or they cannot ever hear the voice of God's spirit calling them into ministry. If one does not have a somewhat exaggerated sense of the seriousness of the problems out there in life, one may not be so conditioned as to be moved by the urgency needed

---

8. Johathan Edwards, *A Treatise Concerning Religious Affections*, Vol. 2, in John E. Smith, ed., *The Works of Johathan Edwards* (New Haven, CT: Yale University Press, 1746, 1959).

9. James, *Varieties*, 34.

10. Karen Horney, *The Neurotic Personality of Our Time* (New York: Norton, 1937).

to sense a call into ministry. This dedication of one's entire life to such self-sacrificial service requires a heightened sense of the need being addressed in ministry. In preparing this chapter, I was pleasantly surprised to notice that William James insists that this quality of normal range neuroticism is necessary, or at least helpful, for anyone's authentic spiritual sensitivity. He insisted that regarding inspiration from God's realm, "it might well be that the neurotic temperament would furnish the chief condition of the requisite receptivity."[11]

He was writing in the context of 19th century "faculty psychology" in which it was assumed that personalities came in four forms: hysteric, dependent, compulsive, and paranoid.[12] These were not intended as terms identifying types of mental illness but as terms describing how various personalities acquire meaning from experience. Hysteric personalities acquire meaning through the drama of life, dependent personalities through relationality in life, compulsive personalities through careful regulation and orderliness, and paranoid personalities through meticulous use of the precise meaning of words. A neurotic personality, presumably, would have a nice balanced combination of hysteric and dependent features, finding meaning in dramatic and relational experiences. James considered this desirable and constructive, because there

---

11. James, Op. Cit., 37.

12. The more familiar set of early psychological categories is Choleric, Melancholic, Sanguine, and Phlegmatic. These constituted the four humors theory of Hippocrates (460–370 BCE) who thought certain human behaviors were related to predominance of certain body fluids in a person's physiological system, i.e., yellow bile, black bile, blood, and phlegm. This notion is not unrelated to the somewhat comparable ancient Greek concept of the constituent elements of the universe: fire, earth, air, and water. The Roman physician, Galen (131–200 CE) developed what was probably the first typology of temperaments in his work *De Temperamentis*, in which he attempted to organize physiological reasons for different human behaviors or personality tendencies. Nicholas Culpepper (1616–1654 CE) was the first to dispense with this ancient idea, but Immanuel Kant (1724–1804 CE) and such other notables as Erich Fromm (1947 CE) theorized on the four temperaments, using different terms for each, and influencing the development in modern psychology of the set of four cited in this text. Hans Eysenck (1916–1997) seems to have been the first psychologist to base his analysis of human personality on a psycho-statistical or factor analysis methodology. Consequently, he concluded, as well, that personality or temperament is biologically based. His categories were Neuroticism and Extraversion, which he perceived as pairing in various degrees, and thus creating patterns similar to the four ancient temperaments of Hippocrates. Modern psychology is increasingly moving to an appreciation of the critical relationship between biochemistry and psychological states.

is always something solemn, serious, and tender about such authentic spirituality and true religion.

It is most interesting that James continues his thoughtful analysis by observing that the other side of this spiritual reality is the fact that authentic spirituality and genuine religion take away the anxieties of life. Fear is not merely held in abeyance by deep spirituality and heartfelt religion, as it is by mere moral achievement. It is positively expunged. The central thing he found in his examination of religious experience was

> how infinitely passionate a thing religion at its highest flights can be. Like love, like wrath, like hope, ambition, jealousy, like every other instinctive eagerness and impulse, it adds to life an enchantment which is not rationally or logically deducible from anything else. This enchantment, coming as a gift when it does come,—a gift of our organism, the physiologists will tell us, a gift of God's grace, the theologians say,—is either there or not there for us, and there are persons who can no more become possessed by it than they can fall in love with a given [person] by mere word of command. Religious feeling is thus an absolute addition to the Subject's range of life. It gives him [or her] a new sphere of power. When the outward battle is lost, and the outer world disowns him, it redeems and vivifies an interior world which otherwise would be an empty waste.
>
> If religion is to mean anything definite for us, it seems to me that we ought to take it as meaning this added dimension of emotion, this enthusiastic temper of espousal . . . It ought to mean nothing short of this new reach of freedom for us, with the struggle over, the keynote of the universe sounding in our ears, and everlasting possession spread before our eyes. This sort of happiness in the absolute and everlasting is what we find nowhere but in religion . . . "It is the infinite for which we hunger, and we ride gladly on every little wave that promises to bear us towards it" (53–56).

James slips the keystone into the finely wrought arch of his argument with a brief summary. The universe and human existence is what it is. The reality of the unseen cannot be disputed by anyone who is aware enough of his or her own nature to have experienced the psychospiritual hunger and quest for the profound meaning of human life. These are those who have experienced the para-psychological and transcendental intimations that entice us to genuine spirituality and authentic religion. Coping with these realities, these givens, in the long run requires that we settle with some renunciation, sacrifice, and surrender. Ultimately we must renounce our notions of being in control and being able to insure our own comfort and security. We are dying persons in generations of dying persons. Along the way we must sacrifice our narcissism and our private, personal claims on having things the way we want them. We must surrender to the process of life from the cradle to the grave, and to the fact that we cannot make meaning out of that process on our own by mere moral character. Finally, mere morality is a container too incomplete and empty to feed the hunger of our spirits for the infinite.

James attempted to categorize all mystical experiences as being of five or six different types. He noted that persons who experience what I have been calling moments of the divine spirit, tend to have a sense of union with that spirit, and sometimes with other humans. Others are conscious of profound illumination, as I experienced at age 7, on the occasion when I heard the voice instructing me to "trust in the Lord and do good," and at numerous other "moments of the spirit" in my life. James also noted that mystical experiences often come in the form of a sense of ineffability when one seems to be taken up into an ethereal state by some dynamic force outside one's will or self. As in the cases I have described as intimations of the spirit in my life and that of many others, James thought that it is not uncommon for persons to experience all these kinds of mystical events in a kind of passive way. They are events that happen to us rather than something we initiate, cause, or create.

Remember the point I made in chapter 5 above on James' observation that many of the persons he interviewed indicated that when they sensed the consciousness of the presence of the spirit it felt as intense as standing in a fulmination of an inner heat source. John Wesley's testimony was the same. When he came to the deep reassurance of God's grace to him, he felt uncommon warmth within. James continued by describing the startling sense of some ineffable good to which his subjects testified, not a standard aesthetic emotion but a certainty of the intimate presence of a mighty person that persisted as the unique perception of reality.[13] The clergyman he cited spoke of the depth of his life-struggle being revealed to him and an unfathomable depth of the transcendent world. As he stood under the stars he was flooded with "the beauty of love and suffering together with a sense of the presence of the creator God. He had not sought it. The spirit came to him and took over his

---

13. James, Op. Cit., 63.

inner self with ineffable joy. It was like an symphony melted into one swelling harmony wafting the soul upwards, and almost bursting it with emotion.[14] There in the quiet darkness he felt a presence more real than his self. He was sure he stood face to face with God.[15]

As I said in chapter 5, these observations ring true to my experience of being filled with an enormous sense of relief and meaning, flooded with the new focus of purpose and calling to ministry, with a life encompassing sense of wellbeing, light that connected heaven and earth, a joyful fullness of the meaning of everything, and utter clarity. Each event changed my life dramatically or drew me into a course of action that changed the life of someone else who badly needed just that, just then.

Most scholars and popular writers who address matters of spirituality testify to the same experience. Moreover, this is not limited to the Christian communities in today's world, but rather tends to be the character of genuinely spiritual communities in all faith traditions. Carl R. Rogers grew up as an Evangelical Christian and later moved away from that conservative perspective, into what he thought of as a basically secular posture of thought and life. Nonetheless, when the time came for him to set down his essential outlook on life, this great psychologist made a number of observations which reinforce the line of thought developing in this chapter.

Rogers asked himself how his life trajectory had unfolded and where it had led him with regard to his view of the objective world of reality. He then observed that the meaning of his journey did not lie in the things that we can see, feel, hold, or possess; nor in the technology with which we are blessed in our day. Neither does it arise, he thought, from the relationships we have with others, or the traditions, organizations, customs, and rituals of the culture with which we identify ourselves. He could not find in logical analysis or theological propositions the essence of what really spoke to his spirit. He did not find that meaning for life even in his own personal world. He found it, he said, in the mysterious and unfathomable realities that lie beyond the boundaries of the tangible world, and are "incredibly different" from it.[16]

---

14. Ibid., 67.
15. Ibid., 67–68.
16. Carl R. Rogers, *A Way of Being* (New York: Houghton Mifflin, 1980).

In an instructive chapter on The Meaning of Spirit, Joseph McMahon, in his book, *Discovering the Spirit, Source of Personal Freedom*, reflects upon the usefulness of such spiritual experiences as this book is about.[17] He remarks, "Although we may be convinced that the reality of spirit underlies our important concerns . . . the reality of spirit comes home to us most forcefully" in personal spiritual experiences.[18] Then he cites two descriptions of spiritual experience from *The Spiritual Nature of Man*, by Alister Hardy.[19]

1) I have had, especially during my childhood, several experiences where I felt strongly that a power in which I could be wholly confident was acting for and around me, even if at that time I was too little to give it a divine explanation.

2) One day as I was walking . . . I was suddenly seized with an extraordinary sense of great joy and exaltation, as though a marvelous beam of spiritual power had shot through me linking me in rapture with the world, the Universe, Life with a capital L, and all the beings around me.

McMahon's insights relate well to the perspective of James and Allport. He indicates that people tend to describe spiritual experiences as intrinsic spirituality, as in the two cases cited from Hardy. In doing so, the descriptions include both sensory and quasi-sensory experiences. They include, typically, visual and auditory events; more the former than the latter. Visual spiritual experiences include what the persons themselves describe as "visions, illuminations, a particular light, and a feeling of unity with surroundings" and with people.[20] Auditory events include voices or music that is designed to have a calming or consoling effect: messages of consolation or guidance. A third set of intrinsic spiritual experiences to which McMahon testifies include healing touch, comforting presence, warmth, reassurance, and the like.

---

17. Joseph J. McMahon, *Discovering the Spirit, Source of Personal Freedom* (New York: Rowman and Littlefield—Sheed and Ward, 1994).

18. McMahon, Ibid., 97.

19. Alister Hardy, *The Spiritual Nature of Man* (Oxford: Clarendon, 1979). See also Hardy, *The Biology of God: A Scientist's Study of Man the Religious Animal* (New York: Taplinger, 1976).

20. McMahon, Op. Cit., 98.

Both Hardy and McMahon operate with a model of ten cognitive and emotional experiences of spirituality that they rank in order of frequency as follows. The higher an experience is on the list, the more frequently it is reported. The first on the list, and thus the most frequently reported is a sense of security, protection, and peace; second, a sense of joy, happiness, and well-being; third, a sense of presence, which is not human but transcendental; fourth, a sense of certainty, clarity, and enlightenment; fifth, a sense of guidance, vocation, and inspiration; sixth, a sense of prayers answered in events; seventh, a sense of purpose behind events; eighth, a sense of harmony, order, and unity in all things; ninth, a sense of awe, reverence, and wonder; and tenth, a sense of new strength in oneself.

Those who described these experiences indicated that they amounted to a new quality of truth and awareness for that person. While Hardy's and McMahon's research indicated that these kinds of spiritual experience occurred most frequently in childhood and adolescence, they were also common in adult life. My own experiences of illumination conform to this pattern. The most dramatic numinous experiences occurred when I was aged seven, twenty three, thirty seven, forty three, fifty, sixty five, seventy two, and at frequent moments of lesser intensity in between. My experiences were life-changing illumination at age seven and at age twenty three; a sense of presence and guidance at age thirty seven, fifty, and sixty five; an audible voice expressing guidance and consolation at age forty three, and an experience of being physical awakened from deep sleep by a strong and repeated rap on the hand combined with or followed by a truly remarkable illuminating sight/vision that set my inner self at ease at age seventy two.

For me all of these experiences were intensely encouraging, consoling, guiding, and affirming. They gave me the sense, in each case, that I was directly in touch with the transcendent world and that the spirit of God was filling the moment with incredible meaning, exactly adapted to the particular need in my life at that time. Hardy and McMahon indicate that the important information they derived from the study was that the *initiative* for the spiritual experience came from inside the respondents themselves and that the *response* to their inner initiative came from transcendent sources, or at least from beyond themselves.

In this regard my own para-psychological or psychospiritual experiences with the divine spirit, throughout my life, have been exactly the opposite, without exception. In every case, for me the initiative came to me from elsewhere, and required no response from me except to savor the gratifying quality of the experience; feeling filled as I did in each case with an immense consoling, clarifying, and illumining presence. It was clear to me in each case that the presence was the presence of a life-filling spirit. I had the direct sense, immediately, without needing to reflect upon it, that it was the divine spirit of God intensely present to me, purposive and transcendent. My type of experience conforms more consistently with the large literature reporting such moments of the spirit than does the data generated by Hardy and McMahon. No one else than Hardy and McMahon that I know of reports these numinous experiences being generated from inside the subject though the description of the experiences is otherwise similar throughout the literature.

That sense of presence was apprehended by me in two dimensions, so to speak. On the one hand, it seemed to be a glow of intense warmth and wisdom and well-being which filled my entire self. On the other hand, it seemed like a glowing celestial aura which took me up into it, as though it had become the matrix within which I was held for the timeless time of the spirit's presence. The residual experience, after the transcendental event or process had passed, was always a sense of strong, very pleasing, and undisturbable well-being. It left me with a sense of relief, security, purpose, direction, consolation, and comfort. I always came away with an awareness of the rightness and coherence of all things in life and the universe: peace with God, my situation, and myself. It settled something central and life-encompassing in my soul.

From my earliest conscious moments I have never had any feeling of being in any way outside of the matrix of God's embrace and the domain of God's spirit, except during the two years of utter darkness from age 5 to 7, when I do not remember feeling anything. The trauma of my early childhood called out for strength and solace that was well beyond me, I am sure. I had known before Esther's death that my parents lived in the world of the spirit. I must honestly say, therefore, that openness to the spirit seemed like a natural part of my life, and expecting its manifestations did not ever seem like something otherworldly or unnatural to daily experience. I think that in our family we just did not think about moments of the spirit. We took that kind of life for granted.

McMahon quotes Hardy describing a similar state as a feeling of oneness which often passed over to a state of listening for the spirit. "I mean by 'listening' that I was suddenly alerted to something that was going to happen. What followed was a feeling of tremendous exaltation in which time stood still. I heard nothing, yet it was as if I were surrounded by golden light and as if I only had to reach out my hand to touch God himself who was surrounding me with his compassion."[21]

I could not put words to my own numinous moments of intimation and illumination that more precisely described my experience than McMahon's words of the last part of that quote: *a feeling of tremendous exaltation in which time stood still. I heard nothing, yet it was as if I were surrounded by golden light and as if I only had to reach out my hand to touch God himself who was surrounding me with his compassion.* In this quote it is interesting, I think, that Hardy and McMahon betray the fact that the experience was often in their case, as it *always* was for me, an event initiated from outside them by the transcendent spirit that came to them to give them the numinous experience. It was not generated from their insides. James confirms this same direction of flow in experiences of the spirit, when he makes the important point that we may have a very real expectation of the presence of God's spirit, and we may prepare for such experiences, but we cannot cause them to happen. God is the ultimate source and cause. The numinous experiences come to us, always as a surprise.

McMahon wondered if there are specific triggers that prompt what he claimed were always intrinsic spiritual processes. Hardy believed his data demonstrated that there were 21 initiating factors from the human side. The most frequently appearing triggers were 1) situational depression and despair, 2) conscious and intentional prayer and meditation on some kind of spiritual content, 3) an experience of natural beauty and its wonder, 4) participation in religious worship of especially meaningful quality, 5) intensely engaging exposure to literature, drama, or film, and 6) illness. These experiences usually produced a new sense of purpose and meaning for one's life, or a new and altered attitude regarding others. I would call these conditions that make us open to the numinous experiences but not the agency, cause, or generator of them. Much of the time such conditions do not eventuate in the numinous experience. Numinous experiences come from the spirit only when the spirit moves to invest our spirits, ready or not.

---

21. McMahon, Op. Cit., 104.

Mystical Spirituality 131

McMahon concludes that Macquarrie and Berdyaev are correct in their perceptions that spirit is not a thing and cannot be objectified.[22] Even when we have had numerous experiences like these modern writers report, and as I have described from my own spiritual odyssey, we cannot identify or describe the spiritual presence as an object or person. McMahon's way of saying it is interesting, "If we really want to know what spirit is we have to be involved in spiritual activities, just as if we really want to know what music is, we have to play music . . . The road to becoming a spiritual person is discovered within ourselves through the spiritual activities of self-reflection, intuition, ultimate choice, and creativity."[23] My experience is that the divine spirit brings to us the life-changing illuminations but McMahon is correct in his point that we do not then retain the objective ability or perception necessary to describe or define that spirit as an object or agent. We are only left with the experience of what it did, does, or the effect it has. Undoubtedly that is why Jesus said, "The spirit blows where it will. You can hear its voice, see its effects, but cannot know whence it comes or whither it goes." When the moment of the spirit is complete it leaves us ignorant of its nature but aware of its work.

As McMahon notes, and as I have described in detail in the introduction to this volume, William James says that spiritual experiences, as we have described them in this work, amount to a shift in energy in our inner person. "What was peripheral in the life of the person, such as God, salvation, and eternal life, becomes central" (104). Rudolf Otto in *The Idea of the Holy* says that in these experiences we are seized by God, confirming what my personal experiences with the divine spirit indicate, namely, that the initiative is from the transcendent side, and not specifically expected or requested, as to time, place, and situation.[24]

On the question why some people experience these events, even frequently or regularly, while others do not, James thinks we develop intellectual inhibitions which keep our spirits in check, preventing the required openness of our inner selves to the divine spirit. This is a failure to trust what we cannot predictably control. I think that may be part

---

22. John Macquarrie, *Paths in Spirituality* (New York: Harper and Row, 1972). Nicholas Berdyaev, *The Divine and the Human* (London: Geoffrey Bles, 1949).

23. McMahon, Op. Cit., 100, 102.

24. Rudolf Otto. *The Idea of the Holy* (New York: Oxford University Press—Galaxy Books, 1958). First published 1923, ninth printing 1966,

of the problem, but I think there is another part to it. I believe that the capacity to recognize the visits of the spirit and to take in the meaning of the events, requires conscious intentionality, on our part, to live life with a spirit open to the transcendental experience: open to these kinds of moments of the presence of God. Then we have eyes to see them and ears to hear them for what they are when they come to us from the divine spirit. The realm of the human spirit and of the divine spirit is sub-rational and sub-volitional, deeper in us than our minds and wills. McMahon says succinctly. "The irony underlying the lives of people that refuse to let go of their rational inhibitions out of fear of losing control is that they get in their own way of reaching a source of power that would give them greater control and direction in their lives."[25]

Abraham Maslow lists numerous characteristics that come to a person from the spiritual experiences we have been discussing.[26] Those which ring true to what happened to me, personally, in the experiences of direct connection with the divine spirit that I have had, are the following. First, the universe seemed, as a result, a coherent unity. Second, I became less ego-centered in my perception of everything. Third, I saw everything in life "under the aspect of eternity." Fourth, the world seemed unqualifiedly good and beautiful. Fifth, I was far more receptive to the divine spirit, more humbly awaiting God's presence, and much more consciously ready to receive the intimations and experience of the spirit than before the numinous event.

We have been concentrating mainly in this chapter on intrinsic spirituality. Philip Sheldrake reminds us that spirituality is not limited to our interior persons and experiences, but also involves our external religious behavior, including biblical studies, theological thought, worship rituals, ecumenical reflection, and sharing of the faith. Such spiritual operations erode obstructive boundaries between people.[27] His book describes the forms spiritual life took in each of the ages of the last twenty centuries in the Western World, heavily influenced by Christianity since the time of Christ himself.

Sheldrake thinks that to describe all these phases of spirituality for the last two millennia requires that we understand the context: the theo-

25. McMahon, Op. Cit., 104–05.

26. Abraham Maslow, *Religion, Values, and Peak Experiences* (New York: Penguin, 1970).

27. Philip Sheldrake, *A Brief History of Spirituality* (Malden, MA: Blackwell, 2007).

logical influences that were prevalent in each age, the forms of worship and liturgical music that shaped the thought and feeling of the congregations, and the large themes shaping history at the time. His main thought about extrinsic spirituality is that the programs and projects which give meaning to the religious practices and spiritual life of many people are more than merely achieving a work objective or following a traditional form of worship. Such religious behaviors embody substantial spiritual wisdom and self expression for the extrinsic person. Patterns of religious behavior are not merely traditions that people keep for their own sake. Frequently, they are or become for such persons deeply meaningful forms of personal communion with the divine spirit because they express a will-full and consciously intentional desire in that person to work out the objectives of the spirit of God, as they understand them and as their traditions of religious behavior have tuned them to do.

One of the most prolific scholars in things related to Christian spirituality and the life of the Christian Church in the world is Alister E. McGrath. In his work, *Christian Spirituality*, he makes a crucial observation that is particularly relevant at this point.[28] He emphasizes that spirituality is closely tied in with the internalization of religious faith. By internalization he means the process of swallowing down into our inner spirits the content of our faith experience, actions, rituals, knowledge, programs, projects, learning, and explorations into the divine spirit.

I say that this perspective is relevant here because it applies equally to the value and fruitfulness of both intrinsic and extrinsic spirituality. McGrath's outlook illumines the development of any person, and of that person's life open to God's presence. He observes rightly that there "need be no tension between an inwardly appropriated faith and its external observance, in that the latter naturally leads to the former." I would add that the extrinsic religious behavior also follows, in turn, from intrinsic experiences of the faith. It is the hermeneutical circle of the human and divine spirit, so to speak.

McGrath cites the pietist movement, and particularly Zinzendorff, to the effect that religious conversion is the wording the Christian community has used historically for describing the internalization of our experiences of deep and genuine spirituality. Zinzendorf was concerned that people should achieve what Martin Luther, the sixteenth century

---

28. Alister E. McGrath, *Christian Spirituality* (Malden, MA: Blackwell, 1999).

reformer, called "the divine work within us." This work renovates us and produces a person with a different heart, spirit, mind, and emotion.

Walter Brueggemann is a notable Old Testament scholar who confirms the foregoing line of thought in his little manual entitled, *Praying the Psalms, Engaging Scripture and the Life of the Spirit*.[29] His point is that using the psalms as devotional reading, to focus our prayer and meditation, results in the psalms being progressively internalized and shaping the perspective and content of our inner awareness of God. What McGrath points out about internalizing the faith specifically confirms the reality of my own experience with the divine spirit, as well as the knowledge I have of my parents' spirituality, and of what I have noticed in the congregations I have served. This rings true for all people of faith and of spirituality, I believe, whether their preferred form of psychospirituality is intrinsic or extrinsic. Having the literature of the spirituality of their traditions extensively internalized by memorization and spiritual appropriation into their personal worldview shapes their inner perspective and expectations regarding the divine spirit.

The most important implication of this empirical reality is the fact that if a person is not tuned to the openness to God that is required for encounters with the divine spirit, and he or she wishes to be, that person can do something about creating that openness. There is a method for setting one's sail close to the wind. It is possible to take Brueggemann's advice and fill one's inner world with the rich spiritual nurturance of the psalms or other biblical theological content. One must be selective, of course. There are psalms celebrating the goodness of God, celebrating the grace and forgiveness of God, imploring the help of God, deploring God's silence, complaining about enemies, and calling down awful things upon one's adversaries. There are healthy psalms, sick psalms, sad psalms, penitential psalms, angry psalms, fear-filled psalms, grateful psalms, and psalms of praise. For the sake of cultivating a wholesome and deep inner spirituality, it is probably a good idea to concentrate upon the first, fourth, and last two types of those mentioned. Those psalms are songs written by persons with lives wide open to the divine spirit, with the sail of life set close to the wind of God's breath.

---

29. Walter Brueggemann, *Praying the Psalms, Engaging Scripture and the Life of the Spirit* (Eugene, OR: Wipf and Stock—Cascade Books, 2007).

Beverly Lanzetta has given this notion a global scope in a book she calls *Emerging Heart, Global Spirituality and the Sacred*.[30] She emphasizes that the human community is now in the birth pangs of a global development in spirituality. This cross-cultural and ecumenical stimulation of spiritual illuminations is creating a new set of spiritual expectations, language, categories, and heart. It is enlarging the spiritual challenge and invitation to all of us to greater openness to the divine spirit in ways that parochial and denominational perspectives cannot offer us.

It is Lanzetta's notion, following her mentor, Ewert Cousins, that in the fifth century BCE, when all at once there appeared upon the cultural, psychological, and religious horizon, Socrates, Confucius, Buddha, Zoroaster, Lao Tzu, the Hebrew Ethical Prophets, and Isaiah, the human ways of thinking about things and experiencing things, mundane and transcendent, were radically and permanently changed. New paradigms were framed for everything. Cousins is sure that we are now experiencing another such global spiritual change, "exemplified by the convergence of religious traditions and a right brain mode of consciousness."[31] He may be right.

He thinks we are making a spiritual paradigm-leap, mutating our consciousness into life that is primarily spiritual and heart-inspired. Lanzetta styles this a "new age unfolding in our midst" that "points toward the emergence of a spiritual renaissance" in the culture on our entire planet. She envisions this new age as one in which a heightening of global spiritual consciousness will usher in a "greater appreciation for the intersection of the sacred and secular."[32] It is not clear that we are near achieving that global spiritual consciousness but it is surely an ideal state for which people of the divine spirit should be delighted to pray without ceasing.

It is gratifying to cite some recent empirical evidence regarding the practical value of cultivating a culture of the Holy Spirit in one's life. Simpson, Newman, and Fuqua undertook empirical analysis of genuine spirituality and psychological health.[33] They observed at the outset that

---

30. Beverly Lanzetta, *Emerging Heart, Global Spirituality and the Sacred* (Minneapolis: Fortress, 2007).

31. Ewert H. Cousins, *Christ of the 21st Century* (New York: Continuum, 1994).

32. Cousins, Op. Cit., 6.

33. David R. Simpson, Jody L. Newman, and Dale R. Fuqua, Spirituality and Personality: Accumulating Evidence, in *Journal of Psychology and Christianity*, Vol. 26,

"generally speaking, research has suggested that more positive spiritual functioning is related to more positive functioning on a variety of dimensions of psychological health." Their study of 190 spiritually mature adults, living life consciously open to the divine spirit, "completed 11 scales designed to measure different dimensions of spirituality, and a measure of the Five Factor Model of personality."

A principal-components analysis indicated that the 11 measures of spirituality could be reduced meaningfully to three underlying components. These components were found to have a substantial relationship with the personality measures. "Generally, the results are consistent with previous research suggesting that those individuals with a healthier spiritual orientation tend to display greater health on personality dimensions as well."[34]

We need not be surprised or triumphalist as a result of this scientific outcome. Such data has been accumulating now for half a century or more. Moreover, persons of the spirit, who have experienced personally the presence and mystical ministries of the divine spirit, have lived with and from this wisdom or knowledge since time immemorial. Rudolf Otto said, in his book noted above, that some of us are tempted to shut our eyes to that which is quite unique in a life lived close to the breath of the spirit of God. But the experiences offered us by the divine spirit are so real and so much a gift that they might as well provoke astonishment and amazement in us rather than merely to give rise to admiration. For if there is any aspect of human experience that offers us spiritual wisdom that is unmistakably specific and unique, peculiar to itself, it is the gifts of a life in the spirit.

Last night my mother and father visited me in a numinous dream. They departed this life in 1993 and 1996 at the advanced ages of 90 and 93, respectively. I have been troubled for the intervening years about the fact that I was not able to attend them more intensely during their final years and that I had not visited them for a considerable time prior to their passing. Unfortunately for me, at least, I was not present at the time of their deaths. It troubles me. When they came to me last night in a spiritual communication they were both their usual kind and peaceful selves; and they did not seem distressed about my having "neglected" them.

No. 1, Spring 2007.
    34. Ibid., 33.

However, they were also not particularly expressive of any special need to console me or give me exciting messages from "the other side." Nor were they especially warm and intimate though that was their usual style. My mother was sitting quietly in a warm and emotive mood, giving the impression that she was feeling pleasant and satisfied that "I had come to see her." She smiled at me and communicated her pleasure nonverbally. My father stood in the doorway, as though he were ready to go on with some useful task, as he usually was, and he carried on a matter-of-fact emotive communication with me that suggested that things were "business as usual." The entire net effect for me was that I came away with the sense that everything was alright as it had always been with us, but that the connection was not in any way remarkably special. I had the distinct impression that this was a first chapter with more to follow. It will be interesting if that proves to be so.

Throughout history people have testified to these kinds of mystical experiences delivered in numinous dreams. An uncle of mine, with whom I was particularly collegial and friendly, lost his wife, my father's sister, a year and a half ago. They were only a decade or so older than I, so we were virtually of the same generation. He was a famous neurologist and board certified psychiatrist. He missed my aunt intensely. Since they had never had children they were exceedingly close to each other, sharing his work, travels, and professional experiences virtually as one person.

Some time after his wife's death, my daughter asked him whether she had come to him since her death. He said she had not but he hoped she would. Some weeks thereafter he reported with an earnest sense of consolation and relief that she had, indeed, come to him in a dream. He said she sat on the edge of the bed and with pleasant assurances told him things were well for her. She said she hoped he would join her soon. She was awaiting him. Within six months he died peacefully in his sleep at 92 years of age. The screen between our conscious state and that state of life after life is permeable and permits communications and visits of persons, just as of the divine spirit.

The world of numinous, illumining experiences is apparently universal with humankind. That which is generally treated as abnormal increasingly seems to be rather normal. The screen between the world of our personal spirits and the pervading spirit in the universe is obviously not a barrier. The numinous experiences range in intensity from moments of remarkable and unaccountable insight, awareness, intuition, ESP, or prescience; to dreams that intimate revelations from other dimensions of existence; and on to life-changing events of illumination that seem to be connections with God and that take us into alternate states of reality while we experience them.[35] We might be tempted to explain the less dramatic ones as merely a mysterious kind of psychological reaction about which we do not yet have adequate information. However, why would we wish to reduce such experiences from what they forthrightly seem to be? My aunt's communication with my uncle and my parents visit in numinous dreams may be taken for what they were experienced to be. Whether the mechanism is primarily psychology, or my grandmother's vision of my grandfather arriving to take her to the other side is some kind of psycho-biochemical reaction of one's dying cerebral extremities is of little import. The issue that is quite obviously in the forefront of those moments of the spirit, is that whatever the channel or mechanism, the divine spirit speaks loudly and clearly, delivering messages of hope, consolation, and joy.

---

35. A number of the ideas and citations in this section of this chapter were previously published in a different form in J. Harold Ellens, *Understanding Religious Experience: What the Bible Says about Spirituality* (Westport, CT: Praeger, 2008), 8–21 and 144–154, and are used here by permission.

11

The Mystics and the Epitome of Mysticism

IN HIS VOLUME ON the psychoanalytic mystics, Merkur entitled his first chapter, The Oceanic Feeling. In its opening pages he describes incisively the nature and scope of mysticism, as he understands it. As noted in our previous chapter, after citing James' reference to mysticism as a sense of union and consciousness of illumination, with lesser features of ineffability, noetic character, transiency, and passivity; Merkur quotes Underhill as saying that "mysticism, in its pure form, is . . . the science of union with the Absolute . . ." Then he describes a more global model of mysticism.

> Recent cross-cultural studies count as mystical not only the unitive and nothingness experiences of Christian contemplatives, Jewish Kabbalists, Muslim Sufis, Hindu yogins, and Buddhist meditators, but also the interior dialogues of prophets, the visionary states of vision questers, shamans, Taoists, and others, and the motor compulsions of spirit mediums and the possessed. To reflect the current trend in comparative surveys, mysticism may be defined as a practice of religious ecstasies (that is, religious experiences during alternate states of consciousness), together with whatever ideologies, ethics, rites, myths, legends, magics, and so forth, are related to the ecstasies.[1]

Merkur continues by observing that many mystical traditions consider the experiences as metaphysical, that is, events of union within God or illumination by the divine spirit that brings a sense of salvific release from life's impasses together with visions of meaning and destiny. It is in this latter sense, mainly, that the life-changing numinous or paranormal experiences are described for our purposes here. Merkur observes that mystical transformation experiences enhance one's sense of self, of

1. Merkur, Op. Cit., 1.

one's empowerment, and of conflict resolution. They may be sought or cultivated by various religious rituals or practices, and by psychoactive drugs. My focus in this volume, as you have noted, is upon numinous experiences that come to us unsought, unrequested, and unanticipated. They seek us out and catch us up in the mysticism of an event initiated by some other agent than ourselves, from somewhere "out there beyond" ourselves. My focus is on one special type of paranormal event in which what I have been calling the divine spirit visits us in a special illumining way.

Merkur continues with a description of the cross-cultural scope of mystical experiences, and their similarity world-wide throughout the ages. At least one third of all adults in the English speaking world report mystical, spiritual, transcendent, or numinous experiences.

> The world's religions regularly consider mystical experiences discontinuous with normal waking sobriety. They are sacred moments, lasting seconds, minutes, or hours, that interrupt otherwise secular experiences of reality. Mystical experiences provide transient glimpses of ordinarily imperceptible spiritual phenomena. The sense of the discontinuity with the commonplace is often heightened by highly positive emotions that may attend mystical experiences: bliss, ecstasy, euphoria, love, innocence, absolution, esteem.[2]

That certainly describes in detail my experiences of the life-changing numinous events that have come to me.

Merkur, himself, perceives that such paranormal experiences are epitomized in what he calls a profound unitive experience. Reviewing some of his identified components or modes of the unitive experience illumines our appreciation of its nature and importance. He speaks first, of the *solitary mode* in which the self is a passive recipient of the experience of serenity, tranquility, peace, and comfort. Secondly, there is the *self-transcending mode* in which a person sees himself or herself, as object viewed from some observation post, so to speak. The *incorporation mode* is that part of the numinous experience in which one feels identified with all reality. The *inclusion mode* locates the bodily self at the center of the unity of all of creation.

---

2. Merkur, Op. Cit., 2. See also Merkur, *The Creative Imagination* (Albany: SUNY Press, 1998); and Merkur, *Mystical Moments and Unitive Thinking* (Albany: SUNY Press, 1999).

He goes on to treat the *identification mode*, the *relational mode*, the *chronological mode*, the *propriety mode*, and the *energetic mode*, in which all reality seems made up of universal energy. The *vitality mode* makes things outside the person seemed to be infused with the presence of transcendent reality, like the divine spirit, in the here and now. The *omnipresent mode* makes everything outside the person seem filled with an omnipresent, divine, and holy power. Merkur continues,

> The *loving mode* imagines self as the recipient of love's loving presence . . . The *omniscient mode* presents self as identical with an intelligent and emotional personality whose knowledge and range of concern are universal . . . The mode of *interior dialogue* involves intrapsychic affects and thoughts that seem subjectively to communicate the feelings and ideas of a personality other than the ego (self).[3]

It is easy to see how these descriptive categories fit the various components that the many different kinds of mystical experiences that are reported in this volume have in common as key elements. These various experiential elements of life-changing paranormal experiences are what psychoanalysis calls the oceanic feeling. Merkur insists that they cannot be reduced to mere psychological regression. He declares emphatically, that "mainstream approach is wrong and should unhesitatingly be abandoned."[4]

Merkur's point throughout his compact volume is that psychoanalysts all use concepts for reality which are mystical in nature. They all imagine an ideal world within or beyond persons, as individuals, that shapes us as we are. Such mystical models include, for example, Freud's imaginative notions of the Id, Ego, and Superego. His colleagues and competitors either agreed with his model or offered alternative concepts of similar mystical nature. These are mythical and mystical models in the sense that it is not possible to actually isolate or get our hands on an object that is the Id, or Ego, or Superego. Their reality is merely posited as a way to talk about some pattern of behavior or function in human personality.

In his imaginative remarks on the healing power of the *Book of Common Prayer*, Schuyler Brown describes the manner in which religious texts and liturgy incite life-changing mystical experiences in the

3. Merkur, *Mystics*, 18–28.
4. Ibid., 29.

devoted worshiper.⁵ Brown believes that the sounds of language, even more than the meaning of sentences, taps directly into the "instinctual hard-wiring" of our inner selves. He quotes Freud's closest ally and firmest critic, Carl Jung, in his remark that the deeper we move toward our unconscious the more we are influenced by sound, "till finally only sound is associated" with our comprehension.⁶ Our use of language seems to order meaning in our minds through the images similar or memorable sounds incite. Brown thinks this is why the emotional effect "of biblical language has to do not only with visual imagery but also with acoustic images."⁷ It prepares the persons inner world for the advent of the spirit in a numinous experience. Quoting Lacan, Brown observes that "the unconscious is structured like language,"⁸ so it should not be difficult for us "to understand why the sound of the English Bible has played such an important role in our religious history," and as the backdrop to mystical spiritual experiences."⁹

> The phonetic links that bind together the linguistic system of the unconscious, enable language to speak directly to the soul. The unconscious web of linguistic associations interacts with emotionally charged patterns of meaning called complexes. Language, as an archetypal reality, stands at the intersection of the psychic and physical worlds, and this is the root of its healing power.¹⁰

We may add that this is also the root of its power to inspire what we have been calling in this volume, the "moments of the divine spirit" encountering us psychospiritually with their numinosity.

Brown says this is the result of the text of the scripture and its reflection in the *Book of Common Prayer*, being a form of communication from God to the believer, at a profound level of the deep unconscious, mediated by the rhythmic and sonorous meter of those ancient docu-

---

5. Schuyler Brown, The Healing Power of the *Book of Common Prayer*, Vol. 2, *Religion*, Ch. 2, in J. Harold Ellens, ed., *The Healing Power of Spirituality, How Faith Helps Humans Thrive*, 3 vols. (Westport, CT: Praeger, 2010), 23–31.

6. Carl G. Jung, *Experiential Researches* (Princeton: Princeton University Press, 1981), 171.

7. Brown, Op. Cit., 27.

8. J. Lacan, *The Language of the Self*, A. Wilden, trans. (Baltimore: Johns Hopkins University Press, 1968), 32.

9. Brown, Idem.

10. Idem.

ments when recited to us in genuinely aesthetic style. I am sure Julian Jaynes would heartily agree. Brown fears that the way the texts give meaning and messages to human beings have been dissected to such an extent by the psychoanalysts and Bible scholars that they have made it almost impossible for us any longer to hear the religious texts speak to our unconscious. The rhythmic sounds of the

> Prayer Book and the King James Bible are effective because they express the *processes of the psyche* more clearly than the *clearest concept,* and enable the hearer to re-experience them [emphasis added]. Before the word becomes the bearer of a concept, it is first of all a [poetic/aesthetic] sound. The banishment of sacred sound from liturgy and scripture breaks the link between the two worlds, between things visible and invisible.[11]

Holy Scriptures set the stage for mystical, numinous, or paranormal experiences by the sense of spiritual authority conveyed by the flavor we savor in the aesthetic art of their language. This is what makes worship speak to the soul. The well chosen words and carefully crafted phrases give to the language of liturgy a tangible quality of markers and symbols of the divine. To achieve that language must have the "immediacy, dignity, and a sense of deep musical rhythm" found in Cranmer's Prayer Book.[12] "The word spoken is the heard word, and what governs acceptability is not only accuracy but euphony."[13] The words must "live on the ear" like unforgettable music to incite the soul to mystical insights and prepare the believer for the visit of the divine spirit in those peak experiences that permanently change one's life. "*The Book of Common Prayer* enshrines the beauty of sacred scripture in the context of Divine worship, and therein lies its healing power" and its inspiration of "mystical moments of the spirit."[14]

---

11. Brown, Op. Cit., 28.

12. Thomas Cranmer, the 71st Archbishop of Canterbury, formulator of *The Book of Common Prayer*, who suffered martyrdom on 21 March 1556, under Mary Tudor, Queen of Scots.

13. Adam Nicholson, *God's Secretaries* (New York: HarperCollins, 2003), 191, 209, 232, 241.

14. Brown, Op. Cit., 30.

12

The Wisdom Book

THE WISDOM A PERSON develops in life depends upon and is shaped by the worldview that is functioning or forming in that person's outlook on life. Each of us is constantly in the process of developing our worldview, that is, the sense of what life and the world means and how the experiences of our lives become meaningful in that context. Moreover, the meaning that our life experiences bring to our outlook on life also constantly reshapes our worldview—our notions of what anything and everything means to us.

We all strive consciously and unconsciously to develop a worldview that is accurate, internally coherent, and true to the realities of the world that stands out there all around us, and that we experience inside our hearts, minds, and emotions. The worldview of each of us is unique—unlike anyone else's worldview, in at least some details. It is possible that a person's worldview might be internally coherent and very convincing, yet be inaccurate and not true to the realities of the world around us. The reason for this is that we see the world around us through the view or perspective that we have decided upon in advance or that we slowly modify as we go along.

If it were my perspective that the earth is flat, it would be easy to develop an entire worldview that is coherent with that, because as I went along in life I would admit into my worldview only those insights that ring true to it. Then I would fill in the rest of the requirements for a meaningful outlook by imagining or speculating about things. So my perspective, in such a case, might be internally coherent and persuasive, but wholly false because I have made a controlling assumption upfront that is completely out of touch with reality. The reality is that this earth is a globe and everything must find its meaning in terms of that. If I start out with basic assumptions that are real I have a better chance for a true worldview. If, in addition, I am wise enough and informed enough to interpret the components of reality and my experience honestly and accurately, I have a very good chance at a genuinely sound worldview.

The assumptions we make at the outset of forming our view of the meaning of life and the world are determined by many things. Our genetic heritage is involved in the sense that it gives us inclinations to like, need, understand, and believe certain kinds of things that someone else might find absurd or irrelevant. Some of us are very left brain dominant and we are genetically predisposed to believe only those things that are rigorously empirical and logical—only things you can see, hear, taste, smell, touch, measure, weigh, and chemically analyze. Such folks miss a lot of meaning that has to do with the inner perceptions of the emotional world that others of us who are right brain dominant seem to have innately. So genetically determined predilection is an important part of the foundational assumptions we formulate in our quest for meaning.

Another factor that is very important is the content of our emotional experience before we are four years old, when we are learning that life or people can or cannot be trusted, life and other people are basically safe or dangerous, life is basically joyful or stressful, peaceful or painful, loving or grievous. The belief system of our parental home usually influences our basic assumptions very heavily, as do the shaping experiences we have in adolescence, and the kinds of relationships we experience as we grow to be adults. Our assumptions are the lenses through which we take in experience as we go along and our experiences all the while also grind those lenses into different shapes as life unfolds for us, so increasingly we see things somewhat differently and our assumptions change.

Thus anyone's worldview may be very true to reality or distorted from reality at any given time. It is, of course, important to have a standard that measures how true is our worldview and therefore how accurate our assumptions are; and how authentic is our continuing interpretation of our experience. That measure is simply the effectiveness with which our worldview works. That is, the measure of accuracy and truth of our worldview has to do with the effectiveness with which our outlook on life manages all the data of learning and experience that makes up our perception of life and the world. The only thing wrong with strict logical empiricism, for example, is that it leaves out an entire world of affective and spiritual data because that data cannot be tasted, smelled, touched, seen with the physical eye, or heard with the physical ear. Spiritual reality cannot be measured in the lab or chemically analyzed but it has profound shaping effects in our lives, nonetheless.

Postmodernism has demanded that we rethink our strictly empirical scientific assumptions and make room for the world of the human psyche and spirit in our total interpretation of life and reality. My worldview, expressed in this book, demands one more thing than that. It asks that we take into consideration also the phenomenological evidence for the palpable operations of the divine spirit in our paranormal experience. I am claiming that the life of the spirit of God within the realm of human life is as real as the empirical fact that water boils at 212° Fahrenheit at sea level on planet earth.

The worldview that I have set forth in this book could be completely wrongheaded, or it could be as true as the whole truth of God, so to speak. It depends upon how well I have built into my interpretation of my life and learning an accurate and honest understanding of my experience and that of all others whose experience I have taken into account. Does my worldview manage all the data of reality as well or better than any alternative worldview? That determines its trustworthiness and truthfulness.

It seems to me that my basic assumptions and my way of looking at life were very heavily shaped by the devout home and genuinely pious society in which I was born and raised. My earliest formation was already shaped by the assumption my parents held that God was very real to us, God's spirit was very active in our lives, and God's providence was the fact of reality that got us through some extremely difficult times and made them meaningful. By divine providence I do not mean, as some think, double predestination or any kind of divine presetting of the events of human life.

I believe providence is always reactive instead of initiatory. By that I mean that God does not cause specific events in our lives, particularly painful and destructive ones, but that God is never absent from them, as in the case of the Wisconsin soldier at Fort Sam Houston, the British Airlines lady in New York, and my dear friend Esther in the remote reaches of northern Michigan. God does not cause but enters into such events to redeem them from utter tragedy and work them around in such a way that they become constructive settings for the moments of the divine spirit to create constructive life-change through them. God fills our pain with his possibilities by turning them into existential moments of the sacred spirit's opportunities. He turns the trash of our lives into fertilizer to make the flowers grow in our spirits.

I consider the numinous illuminations of the divine spirit that we have been discussing in this volume to be a heightened and dramatic level of that divine providence. Providentially these life-changing moments of the spirit existentially address specific needs or opportunities at inadvertent moments of potential life-change. They come at moments that can be made constructive, numinous moments in which the person affected, as a result of some kind of preparatory state of affairs, is or can be open. In this sense, God is not some abstract governing or sustaining force but a personal presence to all of us, as surely as he is to mountain climbers, sea farers, and desert wanderers in extremity, as we reported in previous chapters.

My early formation shaped me definitively with a perspective that expected to see the movement of God's providence and of the spirit's ministry in all aspects of life. I still expect that. The more I learned about the experiences and rewards of faith, the more I studied theology and the biblical testimony to the mighty acts of God in the lives of the ancients, and the more I have reflected on human suffering with parishioners and patients for whom I have cared, the more certain I have become of the truth and relevance of both my spiritually oriented assumptions and my worldview. It made all the difference in the world of the family and community setting in which I grew up, where the spiritual sail was set close to the spirit's wind. I have seen with clarity that we grow only from our pain; and I have observed that the insights we derive from such ordeals can both grow and heal us.

Both the instruction provided by my parents and the church entrenched me in a perspective on the truth that has shaped all of my life. Actually, it must be said that my present day theological outlook and biblical interpretation could not differ more markedly than it does from the traditions of the faith community from which I emerged. That is beside the point. The essential assumptions about the operations of God and God's spirit in the world are still the solid ground of everything for me. I have matured in my understanding of how they work and what to expect from them but that is merely the natural unfolding of a life of faith, thought, trust, inquiry, scholarly research, and experience. As I have made plain in this volume, my inquiry has now come round to a mature fullness in which I can look back and understand clearly much of what it all means about God and about me—about us.

My parents bought a small farm in northern Michigan in about 1924, where my father set up a machine shop. For the next thirty years he farmed and worked in the shop. Unfortunately, he had only just begun to pay off the farm when the depression hit. Moreover, he had loaned all his financial reserve to his eldest brother so he could also buy a farm nearby. The depression put both in jeopardy and his brother went bankrupt. The depression was followed by the WW II, followed by the Korean War, which took three of us sons away from the farm. My father struggled from 1929 to 1949 to pay the interest on the mortgage of his farm. During that time my mother bore nine children, suffered ten spontaneous abortions, and lost two of us to illness in infancy.

I have run into a lot of people in my eight decades who have used such travail as the reason to believe that God is a monster or does not exist. However, what the ordeal did to us as a family was to persuade us that God does not cause those things but enters into them to turn them to our profit. We believed that life is a matrix of radical freedom in which we and all things have the opportunity to make choices and create responsible lives, regardless of the circumstances. In the process there is much inadvertency and the accidents of history.

If there were no mistakes, inadvertencies, and bad choices, that would mean we lived in a clock-work orange, with no authentic freedom. That freedom seemed to us to be a gift of God, not a mistake, and our experience of God in it was that the divine spirit sustained us in hope and trust and averted all evil or turned it to our profit. God entered into those years of pain and fruitfulness and turned my parents into quiet, humble, honorable, and amazingly productive people of God and godliness. They found life very meaningful in it all and, consequently, so did all of us, their progeny.

Life was not easy but it was not without joy. None of us grew up feeling entitled and narcissistic as the culture seems to be today. Moreover, that tone of inherent decency has communicated itself to the generation following us, so far as I can see. Not all of us and our children have the same theological perspective as the tradition of our parents, but all are busy with the quest for faith and truth and meaning. In retrospect it is possible to discern a golden thread of consistent provident care and spirit-inspiration shaping the fabric of our lives, and that whole cloth is regularly decorated throughout with the special life-changing moments of the spirit which I have reported in this book.

I can say without the slightest ambivalence that the Lord has led our lives along in that sturdy providence and spiritual illumination. I have described the significant moment of my call to vocation at age 7. That is just one of the more spectacular moments of the spirit as I see it. God has entered into the painful ordeal of life regularly along the way, turning tragedy into illumination and pain into growth

Two weeks after the terrorist attack on September 11, 2001 my younger brother, Gordon developed an infected tooth. He called his dentist on a Thursday to ask for help. Because Gordon was diabetic the dentist referred him to an oral surgeon who called him on Friday morning to say he could not see him until the next Wednesday but would provide him an antibiotic to carry him until then. Gordon got the Clindamycin from the pharmacist and went into the north woods hunting. Saturday morning he began to bleed from all orifices and developed an intense abdominal disorder. His son took him home, arriving that evening and drove him straight to the hospital because he was already in a coma. The diagnosis was generalized septicemia caused by the Clindamycin which had killed all the protective organisms in his colon and allowed the bug in the tooth infection to run wild throughout his body. By Monday they had resected his colon in a desperate attempt to save his life.

That intervention failed. The family gathered Monday afternoon at 3:00 to discuss terminating life supports. In the middle of those deliberations my brother in law said he had to leave to do an errand for a friend and would be back at 6:00 PM. At the appointed time Orville returned, but on a stretcher, brought by EMS. He had fallen from a roof and was in effect dead of a broken neck and completely destroyed spine. On Tuesday we terminated life supports on both Gordon and Orville at 8:15 AM in the same ICU. There we were, processing the impossible. It all seemed wholly surreal. It was impossible at the time to see any meaning or sense in it, but that does not mean we did not feel the presence of the divine spirit. In a certain sense that was more than usually the matrix in which we held on and carried on and waited for the light.

I need not tell you that it seemed like a long and awful time until the funerals had been arranged and the services had been held and we closed the tombs for both of them. It seemed impossible to move on and I do not think we really did for some time. I, personally, was sure that I would never get over it. Gordon was like a son to me. He was 14 years younger than I and when I shipped overseas as a young soldier he was a child. When I returned he was a young man and was the first to welcome me home. I still have a sense of love for him that goes beyond words that I have ever found to express it.

From the moment we knew he would die, I was fearful that I could never get over his loss and the monstrous manner in which it happened. Subsequently I have discovered that, indeed, I cannot get over it and that I will never get over it. However, the grace of the divine spirit in this for me is the discovery that I do not need to get over it. About a half year after Gordon's and Orville's death I fell into a rather intense, wholly uncharacteristic afternoon nap. I have never really been able to nap or been inclined to nap during the day. I felt an intense heaviness and needed to kick back. I slept immediately and dreamed vividly of Gordon. When I awoke I felt cocooned in a euphoric sense of lightness and illumination with the clear awareness that while I would never get over Gordon's death, I could live with that grief and that it was seasoning me in a way I had not quite felt before.

When I discovered a couple of years ago that my youngest daughter's multiple sclerosis had taken a turn for the worse and that now there was great danger that she would die before me, it seemed like I had been there before. The impending loss of Brenda did not kick me as far down the stairs, so to speak, as had the travail of the loss of Gordon and Orville. Instead it seemed like a life full of grief again, that I would never survive it in the sense of getting over it, but that I would live with its seasoning force. It seemed like familiar territory, terrible but familiar. I began rather to reflect on how this would season me spiritually, as had the death of my brother and brother in law. Mostly, of course, I have felt and continue to feel concerned how this will season Brenda, herself. If it had not been the illumination of the spirit in that afternoon nap, I do not think I could have endured this new tragedy.

It is interesting to me that the spirit brings us moments of the clear sense of our calling, opportunity, duty, or possibilities. These often seem particularly clear in retrospect. As with Moses in Exodus 33, we see the shadow of God's backside, as he has just passed through our lives, so to speak. More rarely the spirit affords us a glimpse into our destiny, as I experienced it at age 7. I believe that I would speak accurately for my parents, and surely for myself in saying that while we have not had many prophetic moments of the spirit that unveiled the future to us, it has seemed automatic to trust that the spirit is certainly going to be present in every future moment when we get into the unfolding future. It has been easy to trust that all will be well.

I remember a poster of a grand mountain scene I once saw in a gothic sanctuary in Germany, that struck me forcibly with its words. It said, in German, "I know so much of God from what I can see that it is easy for me to trust God for the things I cannot see." That rings true for me. Surely this was the radical perception of divine grace and spirit in the enjoinder of Julian of Norwich when she said,

> All will be well,
> And all will be very well,
> And every sort of thing
> Will be very, very well!

Julian of Norwich really got it! That is the way things seemed to me and to my parents all through the ordeal of their lives; and that is certainly how it seems to me every day of mine. In one sense my life could authentically be described as one long gasp of grief. But it never stayed in that channel. It was always, in spite of the ordeal, an intriguing journey in God's providence and in the serendipities of the divine spirit. It is an intriguing experience to keep an eye out every new day for how the spirit will show up around the next corner. When I keep awake to it, the spirit always does show up rather plainly.

When Jesus said that it is necessary to have the eyes to see it, I guess he meant that it depends on the assumptions and perspective with which one comes to each new moment. My assumptions, perspective, and expectations have been enormously fruitful with the intimations of the spirit's presence to me. I think that when we do feel a sense of our destiny, it is always a view seen through the pain we have processed and integrated into the life of our souls by the intimating and illuminating moments of the spirit. Being tuned to the spirit in that way is surely what determines what we are able to see in our experiences, and so recognize as real.

I suppose it is this perspective that has always moved me to tears when hearing the strains of Katherina von Slegel's pensive 17th century hymn, fortunately tuned to the moving strains of Sibelius' Finlandia:

Be still, my soul, the Lord is on thy side.
Bear patiently the cross of grief or pain;
Leave to thy God to order and provide;
In every change he faithful will remain.
Be still my soul; thy best, thy heavenly friend,
Through thorny ways, leads to a joyful end.

Be still my soul, thy God doth undertake
To guide the future, as he has the past.
Thy hope, thy confidence let nothing shake;
All now mysterious shall be bright at last.
Be still, my soul: the waves and winds still know
His voice, who ruled them while he dwelt below.

Be still, my soul, the hour is hastening on
When we shall be forever with the Lord,
When disappointment, grief, and fear are gone,
Sorrow forgot, love's purest joys restored.
Be still my soul: when change and tears are past
All safe and blessed we shall meet at last.

13

Conclusion

Having reviewed key events of my life and having brought to bear upon them various models and corollary narratives to help explain them, it is now more clear to me than ever that paranormal experiences are very normal and universally common for humans. As I wrote this book I began to realize that the life-changing numinous experiences that seem to me to be visitations of the divine spirit come in a variety of ways. Some of the spirit's illuminations and intimations came to me as Direct Revelations (DR) that radically changed my life. This was the case in my illumination at age seven, revealing to me my life's journey, and lifting me out of darkness into relief and exciting expectation. The same must be said for the night time theophony, the voice in the darkness that awakened me, when I was struggling with the anguish of my heresy trial.

Some of my "moments of the spirit" took the form of Inadvertent Providences (IP) as in instances of special intuition, extra-sensory perceptions, and prescience. All three of these aspects of IP seem to have been involved in my anguish during my mother's dying, though I was cognitively unaware of her ordeal and 1500 miles away. Similarly, my prayer for my brother's protection from death in the impending invasion of Japan was an IP. My prayer was unexpectedly answered by the precipitous decision of President Truman to drop the two atomic bombs in August of 1945 and the end of the war in September when my brother was at home on pre-deployment furlough.

I can add at this point, the call to the ministry in the Newton Church. It came in a mysterious manner just in the nick of a time of great need. So also my inadvertent encounter with the young soldier at Fort Sam Houston, the airline hostess in New York, and the like.

A third type of paranormal experiences that definitively affected my life were what I call Conspiring Events (CE). By that term I mean the development of a series of processes, the import of which was unrecognized at the time, which grew to a life-changing confluence of forces that can best be explained as divine intervention. Surely, the illumination that came to me as a result of the tragic deaths of my brother, Gordon, and brother-in-law, Orville, is such a CE. Desperate that I could never get over it, or integrate the loss into my normal life, I was led to a realization that has sustained me in many subsequent loss experiences. That realization was that I *would not* get over such tragedies, but that I *did not need* to get over them. I can live with them, and they are important to the growth and seasoning of my self. As a view from the bridge between time and eternity, I came to see life in a transcendent perspective, to an extent that I had not before. From that I have profited, or been illumined by it ever since. That specifically enhanced my ministry to numerous others whose loved ones I was called to bury.

Another CE is the experience I reported regarding the special initiative at the Troy Presbyterian Church to cultivate a culture of the divine spirit. It raised the congregation's consciousness of the presence of the spirit of God and changed the nature of that church. I would add here as well, Metzger's rejection of my proposed Masters Degree thesis at Princeton conspired to an outcome that was life-shaping and productive beyond my most imaginative expectation.

A final type of life-changing paranormal experiences in my life I call Auspicious Unfolding Outcomes (AUC). I accrued over time, as a result of the minor and major illuminations and intimations of God's spirit in my spirit, a sense of what it means to live life close to the wind. Progressively I learned how to do that and what to hope for or expect from it. Taking that posture toward God with the certainty that the divine spirit is the force of vitality that pervades the entire universe, produced the auspicious unfolding outcome of numerous, spirit induced, changes in my sense of myself, my life's journey, and my hope-filled certitude about the security of my long future with God.

My early formation in a genuinely pious Christian family, our family's utter certainty of the benevolence of divine providence, that setting for my dramatic vocation at age seven, and the assumptions, worldview, and perspective all that generated, conspired to launch me on a trajectory on which the visitations of the divine spirit were not missed. They were able to be, instead, definitive massagers or dramatic shapers of my life. It has been a straight line development from that numinous moment at age 7 to this minute of putting the finishing touches to this book.

When I reached adult life in the scientific university community I set myself upon a course to be a thoroughgoing rational empiricist. I was determined to unscrew the inscrutable with scientific prowess, so to speak. I wanted to make the Bible speak the language of science, as all the major biblical scholars of the time were endeavoring to do, by means of the historical and literary analysis of the texts. However, over the four decades or so of that professional endeavor life overtook me. The spirit impacted my life so dramatically so often that I could no longer account for my experience or for myself without taking into account the numinous peak experiences that were constantly reshaping me. The hound of heaven pursued me down all my days and years. I could not get beyond that divine pursuit.

Finally I settled with an honest and earnest endeavor of explaining the unexplainable in terms of the numinosity the spirit cumulatively brought to my life. The accumulating data was "just there", everywhere in my pilgrimage. It was real, definitive, and not so much requiring explaining as acknowledging and celebrating. Moreover, the life-changes that had accumulated for me along the way were consistently constructive, enhancing my sense of relief, joy, hope, peace, tranquility, meaning, and cognizance of the presence of the transcendent in my mundane daily life.

The unexplainable synchronicities too numerous to recount, the coincidences beyond imagination that were too good to be true, and the inescapable evidence of the permeability of the screen between time and eternity, between the mundane and the transcendent, between my spirit and God's spirit, simply compelled me to give account. Thanks to my friend, Dean Streck, here is the accounting. This book is the celebration and personal report on my life lived with the sail set as close to the wind of God's breath as I could keep it.

Pentecost Sunday 2010
10:10 PM

Bibliography

Atwater, P. M. H. *Coming Back to Life: The After-Effects of the Near-Death Experience.* New York: Ballantine, 1988.

Berdyaev, Nicholas. *The Divine and the Human.* London: Geoffrey Bles, 1949.

Baker, Ian. *A Journey into the Last Secret Place, The Heart of the World.* New York: Penguin, 2004.

Borg, Marcus J. *The Heart of Christianity, Rediscovering a Life of Faith.* New York: HarperCollins, 2003.

———. *Meeting Jesus Again For the First Time: The Historical Jesus and the Heart of Contemporary Faith.* New York: HarperCollins, 1994.

———. *Jesus in Contemporary Scholarship.* Valley Forge: Trinity Press International, 1994.

———, ed. *Jesus at 2000.* Boulder: Westview Press, Division of HarperCollins, 1997.

———. *Conflict, Holiness, and Politics in the Teachings of Jesus.* Harrisburg: Trinity Press International, 1984.

Brinkley, Dannion, and Paul Perry. *Saved by the Light.* New York: Random House, 1994.

Brown, Schuyler. The Healing Power of the *Book of Common Prayer.* Vol.2, *Religion,* Ch. 2, in J. Harold Ellens, ed., *The Healing Power of Spirituality, How Faith Helps Humans Thrive,* 3 vols. Santa Barbara, Denver, London: ABC-CLIO Praeger, 2010.

Brueggemann, Walter. *Praying the Psalms, Engaging Scripture and the Life of the Spirit.* Eugene, OR: Cascade Books, 2007.

Burkhardt, Frederick, and Fredson Bowers, eds. *The Works of William James, The Varieties of Religious Experience.* Cambridge, MA: Harvard University Press, 1985.

Cayce, Hugh Lynn, ed. *Edgar Cayce, Modern Prophet.* New York: Gramercy, 1990.

Chopra, Deepak. *How to Know God, The Soul's Journey Into the Mystery of Mysteries.* New York: Harmony, 2000.

Cousins, Ewert H. *Christ of the 21st Century.* New York: Continuum, 1994.

Edwards, Betty. *Drawing on the Right Side of the Brain.* Los Angeles: Jeremy P. Tarcher, 1989.

Edwards, Jonathan. *A Treatise Concerning Religious Affections,* Vol. 2. In John E. Smith, ed., *The Works of Jonathan Edwards.* New Haven, CT: Yale University Press, 1746 and 1959.

Eliade, Mircea. *Cosmos and History, The Myth of the Eternal Return.* New York: Harper and Row, 1959.

Ellens, J. Harold, *Sex in the Bible, A New Consideration.* Westport, CT: Greenwood-Praeger, 2006.

———. *Understanding Religious Experiences, What the Bible Says About Spirituality.* Westport, CT: Praeger, 2008)

———. *The Spirituality of Sex.* Westport, CT: Greenwood-Praeger, 2009.

———, ed. *Miracles, God, Science, and Psychology in the Paranormal, Religious and Spiritual Events*, 3 vols. Westport, CT: Praeger, 2010.
———, ed. *The Healing Power of Spirituality, How Faith Helps Humans Thrive*, 3 vols. Santa Barbara, Denver, and Oxford: ABC-CLIO Praeger, 2010.
———. *The Son of Man in the Gospel of John*,. Sheffield: Sheffield Phoenix Press, 2010.
Fridrichsen, Anton. *The Problem of Miracle in Primitive Christianity*. Minneapolis: Augsburg, 1972.
Fuller, Reginald H. *Interpreting the Miracles*. Philadelphia: Westminster, 1963.
Fuller, Robert. *Religion in the Life Cycle*. Philadelphia: Fortress, 1988.
Grof, Stanislav. Healing Potential of Spiritual Experiences: Observations from Modern Consciousness Research, Vol. 3, *Personal Spirituality*, in J. Harold Ellens, ed., *The Healing Power of Spirituality, How Faith Helps Humans Thrive*, 3 vols. Santa Barbara, Denver, and Oxford: ABC-CLIO Praeger, 2010.
Hardy, Alister. *The Spiritual Nature of Man*. Oxford: Clarendon, 1979.
———. *The Biology of God: A Scientist's Study of Man the Religious Animal*. New York: Taplinger, 1976.
Henderson, Charles P., ed. "Religion in this Way is Absolutely Indestructible," William James on the Gifford Lectures. *Cross Currents*, Fall Issue, (2003) 464–5.
Hood, Jr., Ralph W., and Greg N. Byrom. *Mysticism, Madness, and Mental Health*, Vol. 3, *Personal Spirituality*, Ch 9, in J. Harold Ellens, ed., *The Healing Power of Spirituality, How Faith Helps Humans Thrive*, 3 vols. Santa Barbara, Denver, and Oxford: ABC-CLIO Praeger, 2010.
Horney, Karen. *The Neurotic Personality of Our Time*. New York: Norton, 1937.
Ingram, Virginia. Evil Experienced by One Who Was There, Vol. 1, *Definitions, History, and Development*, Ch. 4, in J. Harold Ellens, ed., *Explaining Evil*, 3 vols. Santa Barbara, Denver, Oxford: ABC-CLIO Praeger, 2011.
James, William. *The Varieties of Religious Experience*. New York: Morrow; also published in the same year in New York: The New American Library, Mentor Books, 1958.
Jaynes, Julian. *The Origin of Consciousness in the Breakdown of the Bicameral Mind*. Boston: Houghton Miflin, 1976.
Jung, Carl G. *Experiential Researches*. Princeton: Princeton University Press, 1981.
Lacan, J. *The Language of the Self*, A. Wilden, trans. Baltimore: Johns Hopkins University Press, 1968.
Lanzetta, Beverly. *Emerging Heart, Global Spirituality and the Sacred*. Minneapolis: Fortress, 2007.
Lee, E.C.B., and J. E. Elder. *Safety and Survival at Sea*. New York: Giniger-Norton, 2003.
Lenzer, Jeanne. Citizen, Heal Thyself, in *Discover, Science, Technology, and the Future*, September, 2007.
Leslie-Chaden, Charlene. *A Compendium of the Teachings of Sathya Sai Baba*. Prasanthi Nilayam: Sai Towers Publishing, 1996.
Llewellyn, Russ. Religious and Spiritual Miracle Events in Real-Life Experiences, Vol. 1, *Religious and Spiritual Events*, Ch 14, in J. Harold Ellens, *Miracles: God, Science, and Psychology in the Paranormal*, 3 vols. Westport, CT: Praeger, 2008.
Macquarrie, John. *Paths in Spirituality*. New York: Harper and Row, 1972.
Maslow, Abraham. *Religion, Values, and Peak Experiences*. New York: Penguin, 1970.
McGrath, Alister E. *Christian Spirituality*. Malden, MA: Blackwell, 1999.
McMahon, Joseph J. *Discovering the Spirit, Source of Personal Freedom*. New York: Rowman and Littlefield—Sheed and Ward, 1994.

Mendelssohn, Felix. *Elijah, An Oratorio*, Section Number 4, Tenor Aria, New York: G. Schirmer, Inc.

Merkur, Dan. *Explorations of the Psychoanalytic Mystics.* Amsterdam and New York: Rodopi B.V., 2010)

———. *Mystical Moments and Unitive Thinking.* Albany: SUNY Press, 1999.

———. *The Creative Imagination.* Albany: SUNY Press,1998.

Moody, Jr., Raymond A. *Life After Life.* New York: Bantam, 1976.

Morse, Melvin and Paul Perry. *Closer to the Light, Learning From the Near-Death Experiences of Children.* New York: Villard, 1990.

———. *Transformed by The Light, The Powerful Effects of Near-Death Experiences on People's Lives.* New York: Parapsychology Press, 1996.

Newton, Michael. *Journey of Souls, Case Studies of Life Between Lives.* St. Paul: Llewellyn Publications, 2002.

Nicholson, Adam. *God's Secretaries,.* New York: HarperCollins, 2003.

Nouwen, Henri J. *The Wounded Healer.* New York: Doubleday—Image Books, 1979.

Otto, Rudolf. *The Idea of the Holy.* New York: Oxford University Press, 1958.

Restak, Richard M. *The Brain, The last Frontier.* New York: Warner, 1979.

———. *The Brain.* New York: Bantam, 1984.

———. *The Brain Has a Mind of Its Own, Insights From a Practicing Neurologist.* New York: Harmony, 1991.

———. *The Modular Brain.* New York: Scribners, 1994.

———. *Receptors.* New York: Bantam, 1994.

Rogers, Carl R. *A Way of Being.* New York: Houghton Mifflin, 1980.

Ryrie, Charles Caldwell. *The Miracles of Our Lord.* New York: Nelson, 1984.

Schleiermacher, Friedrich D. E. *Glaubenslehre.* Berlin: Jacob Frierics, 1830/31.

———. *Die Praktische Theologie nach den Grundsäzen der evangelischen Kirche.* herausgegeben von Jacob Frerichs. Berlin: De Gruyter, 1983.

Sheldrake, Philip. *A Brief History of Spirituality.* Malden, MA: Blackwell, 2007.

Simpson, David R., Jody L. Newman, and Dale R. Fuqua. Spirituality and Personality: Accumulating Evidence, in *Journal of Psychology and Christianity*, Vol. 26, No. 1, Spring, 2007.

Smart, Ninian. *The Religious Experience of Mankind.* New York: Scribner, 1969.

Smith, Christian. Are You Experienced? in *Books and Culture, A Christian Review*, Vol.16, No. 3, May/June 2010, 14–15.

Springer, Sally P. and Georg Deutsch. *Left Brain, Right Brain.* New York: Freeman, 1981, 1985.

Suedfeld, Peter, and John Geiger. The Sensed Presence as a Coping Resource in Extreme Environments, in Vol. 3, J. Harold Ellens, ed., *Parapsychological Perspectives*, Ch. 1, in *Miracles: God, Science, and Psychology in the Paranormal,* 3 vols. Westport, CT: Praeger, 2008.

Taves, Ann. *Religious Experience Reconsidered, A Building Block Approach to the Study of Religion and Other Special Things.* Princeton: Princeton University Press, 2009.

Theissen, Gerd. *The Miracle Stories of the Early Christian Tradition.* Edinburgh: T&T Clark, 1983. Originally published as *Urchristliche Wundergeschichten: Ein Beitrag zur formgeschichtlichen Erforschung der synoptischen Evangelien.* Gutersloh: Gutersloher Verlaghaus Gerd Mohn, 1974.

Underhill, Evelyn. *Mysticism: A study in the nature and development of man's spiritual consciousness*, reprinted in 1955. New York: New American Library, 1910)

Vincent, Ken R. *Visions of God from the Near Death Experience.* Burdett, New York: Larson Publications, 1994.

Wilber, Ken. *The Spectrum of Consciousness,.* Wheaton, IL, Madras, London: The Theosophical Publishing House, 1977.

———. *The Atman Project, A Transpersonal View of Human Development.* Wheaton, IL, Madras, London: The Theosophical Publishing House, 1980.

———. *No Boundaries, Eastern and Western Approaches to Personal Growth.* Boulder and London: Shambala Press, 1981.

Wilson, William P. How Religious or Spiritual Miracle Events Happen Today, Vol. I, *Religious and Spiritual Events*, Ch 15, in J. Harold Ellens, ed., *Miracles: God, Science, and Psychology in the Paranormal.* Westport, CT: Praeger, 2008.

Subject/Name Index

Allport, Gordon, 127
Amos 7:12, 51
Aquinas, Thomas, 59
Augustine, Aurelius, 59
Atwater, P. M. H., 33
Auspicious Unfolding Outcomes (AUC), 154
Baker, Ian, 42, 46
Bion, Wilfred R., 118
Book of Common Prayer, 141–43
Borg, Marcus J., 114
Bowers, Fredson, 120
Brinkley, Dannion, 34
Brown, Schuyler, 141–43
Brueggemann, Walter, 134
Bultmann, Rudolf, 81
Burchardt, Frederick, 120
Byrom, Greg N., 19
Casey, Edgar, 50–60
Chopra, Deepak, 50, 59–61
Conspiring Events (CE), 154
II Chronicles 9:29–31, 12:13–16, 29:1ff, 35:15, 51
I Corinthians 15, 31
Cousins, Ewert, 135
Cranmer, Thomas, 142
Deutsch, Georg, 55
Direct Revelation (DR), 153
Dunne, Dominick, xiv
Edwards, Betty, 55
Edwards, Jonathan, 122
Eigen, Michael, 119
Eliade, Mircea, 88–90
Ellens, Brenda L., 82–85, 150
Epstein, Alice, 23–24
Exodus 33, 150
Fredrichsen, Anton, 24
Fromm, Erich, 118

Fuller, Reginald, 24
Fuller, Robert, 20
Fuqua, Dale R., 135
Geiger, John, 94–103
Grof, Stanislav, 14
Groom, Michael, 99
Grotstein, James S., 118
Hardy, Alister, 127–34
Hasten, Dougal, 98
Heater, Gabriel, 69
Henderson, Charles P., 119
Herzog, Maurice, 98
Hillary, Sir Edmund, 98
Hillary, Peter, 100
Hillman, James, 119
Hood, Ralph W., Jr., 19
Horney, Karen, 122
Inadvertent Providences (IP), 153
Ingram, Virginia, 94
Isaiah 29:10, 50:1ff, 51
James, William, 52–62, 88–90, 118–34
Jaynes, Julian, 54–60, 104–5
Jellema, Harray, 50
Jesus of Nazareth, 12
Jimeno, Will, 100
Joel 2:28, 52
Julian of Norwich, 59, 151
Jung, Carl, 142
Kelsey, Morton T., 37
Kennedy, John F., 8
Ketchum, Wesley, 58
Kohut, Heinz, 118
Kubler-Ross, Elizabeth, 28, 34
Kukuczka, Jerzy, 98
Lacan, J., 142
Lanzetta, Beverly, 135
Lee, E. C. B., 100
Lee, Kenneth, 100

Subject/Name Index

Lenzer, Jeanne, 21–24
Leowald, Hans N., 118
Leslie-Chzadin, Charlene 60
Lewis, Clive Staples, xi, 70
Lewis, David, 99
Lindberg, Charles, 100
Lindemann, Hans, 99
Llewellyn, Russ, 41–42
MacArthur, Douglas, 68–69
Maslow, Abraham, 132–34
Matzke, John, 21–24
McGrath, Alister E., 133–34
McMahon, Joseph, 127–35
Mendelssohn, Felix, 52
Merkur, Dan, 118–148
Messner, Reinhold, 98
Metzger, Bruce M., 70, 80–83
Micah 3:7, 51
Milner, Marion, 118
Moody, Raymond A., Jr, 27–34, 97
Morse, Melvin, 36
Newman, Jody L., 135
Newton, Michael, 36–37
Nicholson, Adam, 143
Nouwen, Henri, 112
Otto, Rudolf, 88, 89, 131, 136
Paranormal, 10, 16, 19–21
    Experiences, x, xiv–xvi, 14–19
    Events, 14, 86
    Science of, 16–18
Parapsychological, xiv, 25
Parker, Alan, 100-1
Perry, Paul, 34–36
Piper, Otto, 81–82
Presence, xi, 49, 94–103
Proverbs 18:24, xvii
Psalm 37:3, 77
Ralston, Aron, 100
Rank, Otto, 118
Ranken, Henry William 118
Restak, Richard, 55
Rogers, Carl R., 126
Romans 8, 78
Ryrie, C. C., 24
Sathya Sai Baba, 59–60
Schleiermacher, Friedrich 89
Scott, Doug, 98

Shackleton, Sir Ernest 100
Shaver, John L., 6
Sheldrake, Philip, 132–34
Simpson, David R., 135
Slocum, Joshua, 99
Smart, Ninnian, 88–90
Smith, Christian, 87–92
Smyth, Frank, 96
Spirit, Divine, x, 5, 8, 12, 50, 92, 118
    Holy, xv, 8, 13, 48, 86–87, 92
    Culture, 12, 13
    Illumination, 14, 71, 84, 149, 153–55
    Intimations, 117–18, 153
    Wind of the, 47–64, 155
Springer, Sally P., 55
Stob, Henry, xiv
Streck, Dean, xiii, xiv, xix, 155
Suedfeld, Peter, 94–103
Symington, Neville, 118
Tavis, Ann, 87–92
Theissen, Gerd, 24
Truman, Harry S., 69
Türa, Enzio, 99
Underhill, Evelyn, 119
Van Houten, Esther, 1–4, 40, 75, 102
Vidal, Gore, xiv
Vincent, Ken R, 38
Von Slegel, Katherina, 151
Wesley, John, 53
Wilber, Ken, 60
Wilson, Maurice, 97–98
Wilson, William P., 21
Winnicott, D. W., 118
Wisdom Book, xiii

www.ingramcontent.com/pod-product-compliance
Lightning Source LLC
Chambersburg PA
CBHW051932160426
43198CB00012B/2118